Get Your
Sh*t Together

Also by Sarah Knight

THE LIFE-CHANGING MAGIC OF
NOT GIVING A F*CK

Get Your Sh*t Together

How to stop worrying about what you should do
so you can finish what you need to do
and start doing what you want to do

Sarah Knight

Quercus

First published in Great Britain in 2016 by

Quercus Editions Ltd
Carmelite House
50 Victoria Embankment
London EC4Y 0DZ

An Hachette UK company

A CIP catalogue record for this book is available
from the British Library

HB ISBN 978 1 78648 408 6
TPB ISBN 978 1 78648 410 9
EBOOK ISBN 978 1 78648 409 3

Illustrations and hand lettering by Lauren Harms

10

Printed and bound in Great Britain by Clays Ltd, St Ives Plc

Author's note

Hello, and welcome to *Get Your Shit Together*. Thanks for reading! Before we get too deep, I wanted to clarify a few things.

First, despite the real or virtual aisle you may have found it in, this is not a traditional self-help book.

It's more of a let-me-help-you-help-yourself-help book, with "me" here to "help" when your "self" gets in the way. Let's face it — if you could help yourself, you'd have done it by now, right? Also, unlike many traditional self-help authors, I am going to use the word *shit* 332 times (including several *shitmanteaus* of my own invention), so please do not go on Amazon saying you were expecting sunshine and kittens and got shitstorms and shittens. My mother reads all of those reviews and it really upsets her when people don't "get" me.

Second, although your life may be a mess — and I will help you sort it out — this is not a typical guide to "tidying up."

We won't be spending the next three hundred pages gathering your physical shit into a pile and thanking it for its service before you ship it all off to the Salvation Army. Instead, we're going to tidy up your *mental* clutter and your *metaphorical* shit — such as your career, finances, creative pursuits, relationships, and health — and we're going to do it all without hoisting a single trash bag or having an introspective conversation with a winter coat.

Finally, just to be 100 per cent clear: If you were looking for tips on scat play, *this is not the book for you.*

I'm not judging! I simply want to manage expectations. That's what authors' notes are for.

So what IS this book? Well, I think of it as a delightfully profane one-stop shop for tidying your mind — and making your life easier and better.

Like, a *lot* easier and better, no matter where you're starting from.

You may be literally lying on your couch, sitting at a

bus stop, or dangling your feet from the Herman Miller Aeron chair behind your big shiny desk — but I'm guessing you picked up this book because, figuratively, you're in somewhat of a rut. And there's no shame in that. Ruts (even literal ones) are easy to fall into. People do it all the time.

Yours could be shaped like a pair of comfy sweatpants and filled with stale Stella. It might be lined with the silvery stock options you stand to cash in if you can just stick with your soul-killing job for five more years. Or maybe — and this is probably more likely — your rut takes the form of the regular old daily grind: work and finances and family and friends and a lot of other shit you need help staying on top of, plus neglected health (and even more neglected hobbies), and capped off by the dreams you only admit to friends after a few cocktails…or are too scared or anxious or overwhelmed to admit to yourself at all.

Sound familiar? Well, then, strap in! Because this little let-me-help-you-help-yourself mental tidying guide can hoist you out of your rut and drop you slap-bang into the life you want, and deserve, to live. (In a pinch, you could lay it in an actual rut and step on it to keep your shoes from getting all muddy. But maybe save that for after you read it.)

Get Your Shit Together shows you how to set goals, how to push through small annoyances and thorny obstacles to meet those goals, and then how to imagine and achieve even bigger goals that you may not, until now, have thought possible. It will help you get out of your own way, and stay out. And it will liberate you from the shit you think you *should* be doing so you can bang out the shit you *need* to do, and get started on the shit you *want* to do.

How's that for managing expectations?

Basically, this book will do for your life what Tim Ferriss did for the workweek—break it into small, manageable chunks that leave you with plenty of free time to pursue your dream of becoming a self-satisfied entrepreneur/public speaker/sociopath.

No, I'm kidding. But it will do that first part, if you keep reading.

Contents

11

SMALL SHIT: Nailing down the day-to-day to build a better future 55

|||

TOUGH SHIT: Getting older, getting ahead, getting healthy, and getting better at life in general   139

IV

DEEP SHIT: Mental health, existential crises, and making big life changes   **221**

Get Your
Sh*t Together

Introduction

We all have our *Oh shit* moments.

They can happen when we compare the balance in our bank account to the balance on our credit card and find out what "overdraft protection" was meant for, or when we pull on our favourite pair of pants and realize they didn't fit two sizes ago. Or maybe when we wake up next to our formerly favourite person and realize he or she didn't fit two *years* ago.

Yikes.

My most recent one of those moments came when I realized that the reason I was so unhappy all the time was because I didn't love my job any more—and not just *that* job with *that* company, but really an entire career I no longer wanted to devote my life to. It wasn't pretty. And it was followed by a bunch more moments of "What the fuck am I going to do?" and "How the fuck am I going to do it?" before I was able to get out of my hamster-on-a-wheel-shaped rut and start making a few Big Life Changes.

Now I'm here to show you how you can make some big changes too. Or small ones. Whatever you need to do to be happy.

Honestly? You just have to get your shit together.

Again, I'M NOT JUDGING. It's completely understandable why change (of any size) hasn't yet made it onto your to-do list. It's one thing to have an *Oh shit* moment, but it's quite another to actually *do something about it.* Especially if you're the kind of person who has no idea where to start. Or maybe you have no trouble getting started, but you tend to lose steam before you finish—there's too much to do and not enough time to do it, and even if you could do it all, for fuck's sake, how do you avoid driving yourself crazy along the way?!?

I assure you, it's possible.

Getting, having, and keeping your shit together enables you to experience potentially life-changing realizations and then move forward to the "doing something about them" and "not going crazy" side of things. It's kind of amazing. And none of this stuff is as hard as you might think — all it takes is a different way of thinking about and doing shit than you might be used to.

A better way. An *easier* way.

And it works whether you're an overwhelmed underachiever or a high-functioning basket case. Believe me, I know from experience.

A couple of years ago I was so depressed that I could barely get out of bed in the morning. I dreaded the prospect of walking out of my door to get on the subway, because the subway took me to a place that had started to feel less like an office and more like a Temple of Doom. I'd had these feelings for at least a year before *that,* and they were translating into Major Daily Freakouts, but I'd spent fifteen years clawing my way up the corporate ladder — I couldn't jump off it now just because I was feeling a little blue, could I? I had to stay committed even if I didn't love it any more, given all the time and energy I'd already put in… right? (Hint: NOPE.)

It took me far too long to figure out that **there was so much more I** *could* **be doing with my life, if I could only stop worrying about what I** *should* **be doing.**

And I would consider it an honour to save YOU a bunch of time fighting with yourself over staying in bed (or in credit card debt, a bad relationship, or elastic-waist pants) instead of facing reality. Because once you face reality, you can start bending it to your will.

That's what happens when you have your shit together.

Once I identified what I really wanted — to work for myself and attend precisely zero meetings per day — I never looked back. Not only did I quit my safe, steady corporate job to take the risk of going freelance, I had another realization: that being a freelancer would allow me to "commute" from anywhere. Not just my couch in Brooklyn, but perhaps by the side of a pool in the Caribbean.

And oh, wait, maybe I could just move to the Caribbean. That would be nice too, wouldn't it?

So I did it — and in part I, I'll show you how it all played out.

But listen, I don't want to scare you off. Those were some 100 Per Cent Certified Big Life Changes, and like I said, *Get Your Shit Together* can help you make plenty of smaller ones too.

For example, do you ever find yourself stuck at the office — or just glued to the couch — when what you really want is to get out (for once), get to the gym (at last), or get started on that "someday" project that's been hanging out on your to-do list since, oh…the beginning of time?

We've all been there. We've all reached the point where we just can't do any more work or face any more smug Pilates instructors or conceive of cramming an Intro to Portuguese class into the only free afternoon we've had all month.

Of course, we also all know people who seem to breeze through life effortlessly kicking ass and taking names; who always have a plan, are laser-focused on the details, and whose to-do lists exist in a perpetual state of *done, done, and diggity-DONE*. Nine of them are probably superhuman robots built by the government, but I'm willing to bet the rest could use some help getting their shit together too.

In fact, maybe that person I just described — the one

with a jam-packed calendar full of high-power lunches — maybe *that's* you. And maybe you're starting to realize those long hours aren't worth the ivory card stock your fancy business cards are printed on. That the company softball games and charity 10Ks that have consumed your weekends for a year are why you haven't eaten dinner with friends in about as long as those same friends have had "learn Portuguese" on their to-do list. (They all hate you a little bit, but they don't know you're struggling too.)

What would you say if I told you that **there's a path straight down the middle for all of us,** leading right to the lives we want to live? It's true! This book has something for everyone:

Tips for becoming better organized, motivated, and on time? **Check.**

Tricks for saving money, setting boundaries, and having difficult conversations with friends, family, and colleagues? **Double check.**

How about advice for transcending everyday bullshit so you can finally focus on big-time dreams, like changing careers, buying a home, or just moving out of your parents' basement? **You. Are. In. Luck. It's all here.**

I know what you're thinking. *How could so much goodness be contained in such a compact volume?*

This is a valid question. The answer is: I'm not here to teach you how to do a million separate things—there isn't enough hand sanitizer in the world for that kind of handholding. I'm here to show you **how to *approach* all the different stuff in your life so you can get it done in your own way, on your own schedule.** My methods apply to all kinds of shit. And as it happens, I've had some success helping people make changes in their lives using simple advice, a bunch of expletives, and the occasional flowchart.

My first book, *The Life-Changing Magic of Not Giving a Fuck,* was about **how to stop spending time you don't have with people you don't like, doing things you don't want to do.** The *New York Times* deemed it "the self-help equivalent of a Weird Al parody song" and the *Observer* magazine anointed me an "anti-guru." Probably none of this was what my parents had in mind when they sent me off to Harvard, but that's where we are. People all over the world felt the burden of giving too many fucks, and I helped lift that burden by showing them how to give fewer, better ones.

Of course, I also said things like "Sometimes it's okay to hurt people's feelings" and "Wear a gimp suit and sequined heels to your performance evaluation and immediately become the Mayor of No Fucks Given." So, yeah, I guess *anti-guru* suits me just fine. Maybe I'll get a plaque for my lounge chair.

Anyway, if you've read that book, you know about my crusade for **mental decluttering.** (If you haven't read it, well, I don't want to be gauche, but there are plenty of copies in circulation.)

Mental decluttering crash course

Like decluttering your physical space, mental decluttering takes two forms: **discarding and organizing.** In order to give fewer, better fucks — to get the most out of your limited time, energy, and money — you have to **discard** the obligations (or things, events, people, etc.) that annoy you, thus making room

---

for the ones on which you are delighted to spend all your time, energy, and money. That's called **"making a Fuck Budget,"** and I highly recommend it.

Getting your shit together is **organizing** what you have left (in the form of time, energy, and money) and **deploying those resources wisely** — not only on things you *need* to do, but on those extra bonus-level things you *want* to do and just can't seem to afford or get around to. Big change, small change, whatever. It doesn't start with cleaning out the garage. **Change starts with cleaning out your mind.**

Fortunately, **tidying your mind is a solo mission.** If you live in a home with family or roommates, their physical clutter becomes your physical clutter. You have to compromise about how many limited-edition Pez dispensers get displayed on the mantel and which ratty old hotel slippers qualify as "keepsakes" from your honeymoon. Whereas with mental decluttering, you don't have to sort through or trip over anyone's shit but your own. Even if you live on a Disney cruise ship with 7,000 other people (which I sincerely hope you do not), you have complete and total dominion inside your own head. You are judge, jury, and execution—er, on second thought, you're the boss.

In short: *needing* or *wanting* to give a fuck about something is not the same as actually *being able to do it*. For that, you also need to have your shit together.

For example, you may give a fuck about taking a ski vacation and be willing to devote your time and energy "fuck bucks" to the cause, but if you don't have your shit together, you may not have any *actual* bucks to pay for it. You can clear your calendar of less appealing obligations all you want (Who gives a fuck about "Take Your Child to Work Day"? Not you!) — but without funding, you'll be spending your vacation playing old-school Nintendo *Slalom* from your futon.

Or maybe you've decided that what's really important in life is having a deep-soaking tub, and you're ready to say "Fuck that skinny shower stall that forces me to shave my legs like a contortionist flamingo!" In this hypothetical, you have the funds with which to make your Calgon-scented dreams come true, but you lack the gumption to get started. You allegedly give a fuck about ease of use, comfort, and bubble baths — but the soaking tub situation is going to require a full bathroom renovation and you don't have the wherewithal to start a big project (hire a plumber, choose a tub, make arrangements to pee somewhere else for two weeks while the work gets done). Instead, you just keep banging your elbows on the shower door every time you reach up to shampoo your hair.

We can work with this. *Get Your Shit Together* covers

- Who needs to get their shit together, and why

- Three simple tools for getting (and keeping) your shit together

- The Power of Negative Thinking

- How to get out of work on time and save money while you're at it

- Managing anxiety, avoiding avoidance, and conquering your fear of failure

- Making Big (and small) Life Changes

- And tons of other awesome shit!

And although I will tell you how I did it (because it's an instructive example of getting your shit together), I promise this book isn't just a thinly disguised guide to quitting your job and moving to the islands — I'm not sitting here trying to push my life choices on you like some goddamn vegan. You might be someone who enjoys "steady paychecks" and "the rustle of autumn leaves" and whatnot. Or you may be working toward smaller changes, or more amorphous ones. It's all good. I'm just here to help you access the simple, universal wisdom of getting your shit together, for which I happen to be a convenient and willing conduit.

It's worked on my husband; I see no reason it can't reach a broader audience.

Oh, and one more thing:

In this book, "Get your shit together" is not an admonition.

It's a rallying cry.

I admit, sometimes I find myself muttering those four little words under my breath in a somewhat, shall we say, exasperated fashion. You probably do too. For me it's usually at people who show up late and offer completely transparent excuses; at friends who complain about the exceedingly predictable consequences of their terrible life choices; or at fellow passengers who think *I guess I'll just sit wherever* is a viable strategy for ticketed airline travel.

This book acknowledges that most of us *are* those people — if not always, then at least once in a while. I mean, you should have seen me trying to file my taxes last year. It was like the blind leading the blind leading a drunk toddler. Mistakes were made.

But ultimately, I have my shit together about 95 per cent of the time (my comprehension of federal tax code notwithstanding), and you can too. Before now, you may have been too busy getting in your own way, but I assure you, the potential and the tools are there. I'll show you where it is and how to use them.

When we're finished, you'll have *your* shit together — and then maybe you can write a book about how to file your motherfucking taxes like a goddamn adult, and I'll be first in line to buy it.

Deal?

Fantastic. **Let's do this shit!**

1

What we talk about when we talk about getting your shit together

We're going to ease in by shoring up the fundamentals.

First, I'll identify **who needs to get their shit together and why**, which includes a fun story about losing my entire net worth in a New England mall. Next, I'll explain my philosophy on **"winning at the Game of Life."** (It's not the Charlie Sheen version. Not only did that guy give winning a bad name, he managed to get fired from the number-one-rated network sitcom while he was at it.) Then I'll walk you through **the first of many detailed examples of getting your shit together,** and show you how **life is like an adult colouring book.** If you play your cards right, there may even be an ACTUAL COLOUR-ING EXERCISE in it for you.

Like I said, one-stop shop.

Finally, I'll introduce you to a very important concept — **The Power of Negative Thinking** — and reveal how **three little everyday tools** can help you get your shit together.

You may be surprised to learn you've had them on you all along.

Who needs to get their shit together — and why

Fortunately for *moi*, lots of people need this book. They walk among us every day, dropping their phones in toilets, forgetting to pay bills, going to job interviews dressed like they're auditioning for *Strictly*. Such folks include but are not limited to: your friends, family members, classmates, and coworkers; total strangers; and one guy who asked me to send a free autographed copy of my first book to him in Morocco because he can't find it there and also can't afford return postage. That guy needs a straight-up one-on-one tutorial.

But no matter who you are, **let it be known that not having your shit together doesn't automatically make you a bad person.**

True, Justin Bieber doesn't have his shit together and odds are he's a bona fide jackwagon, but that's a special case. (Call me, Justin!) For most of us, not having our shit together is merely **an inconvenient state of being,** not a true character flaw. And the good news is that unlike other potentially unsavoury states of being, such as "too short" or "from Texas," it can be altered without steel rods or forged birth certificates.

So who are you and in what ways is your shit lacking togetherness? Let's take a look at that spectrum, by way of three recognizable cultural archetypes known as "Alvin and the Chipmunks."*

THEODORE: Relatively hopeless

The youngest of the performing chipmunk brothers, Theodore is sweet, agreeable, and naïve. He's along for the ride, but never, ever in the driver's seat. Like Theodore, some people just can't get it together, period. Full stop. They're constantly spilling on themselves (and others), losing their (and other people's) possessions, and **making life far more difficult for themselves** (and everybody else) than it needs to be.

These are the folks — however nice and well intentioned they may be — who are chronically late, underprepared, and

---

* First appearing on American television in *The Alvin Show* in 1961, these lovable singing rodents gained popularity through their 1983–1990 cartoon *Alvin and the Chipmunks,* as well as subsequent globally released live-action films with sequels still being produced as of this writing. Quite the franchise.

overwhelmed. They have to open their suitcases at the airline check-in desk to take out two pairs of shoes, a souvenir mug, and a jar of beach sand that caused their bags to exceed the weight limit. Then they have to frantically figure out how to get this stuff on the plane before everybody in line behind them revolts. If you are a Theo-

Shit Theodores may need help getting together

Showing up on time
Following directions
Remembering where they
    put stuff
Keeping their calendars
    up-to-date
Actually owning a calendar

dore, fear not—every day doesn't have to be an epic battle. Read on.

ALVIN: Cruises along just fine, but is unable to kick it into high gear

The eldest chipmunk is fun and he talks a good game, but he doesn't plan very far ahead, which frequently gets him into trouble. Alvin's kind of a "fake it till you make it" guy, where the ratio of *making it* to *not making it* is weighted toward the latter. When the going gets tough, it's usually his own damn fault—and then he bails, initiating the famously exasperated "Alllllllllvin!!!" refrain from his adoptive human dad/manager, Dave. (They're a cartoon family; don't overthink it.)

Alvins — the humans, not the chipmunks — skate by on the day-to-day stuff, but when it comes to doing shit on a larger scale, they falter. These people arrive home from a relatively productive day at work and make dinner in the microwave because the oven door has been broken for three months and they haven't got around to dealing with it. Or they can totally manage a fantasy baseball team, but when it comes to planning for retirement it's as though numbers and statistics cease to have meaning. Finally, Alvins make the rest of us — bosses, colleagues, friends, backup singers, etc. — nervous. We're like *He seems cool, but can he be trusted?* Eventually the chances run out, the opportunities dry up, and you're just another boy band casualty.

It doesn't have to be this way. If you Alvins have your shit together a little bit, you can get your shit together for the

Shit Alvins may need help getting together

Hitting deadlines on purpose rather than by accident
Sticking to a budget
Sticking to a diet
Event planning
Planning anything more than a week in advance

big stuff, I promise. You're just a dash of discipline and a pinch of willpower away from legendary baller status.

SIMON: Keeps up appearances while dying from a thousand self-inflicted cuts

Finally, there's Simon. Middle sibling, chess wizard, rocks glasses and a blue turtleneck. He's always prodding Theodore, cleaning up after Alvin, and generally doing more for the family than Michael Corleone.

Simons are objectively industrious and successful and know how to operate a suitcase. In their fully functional, chef's-quality ovens, they roast chickens on the regular. They plan elaborate shindigs, never say no to a friend in need, and are very, very good at Excel spreadsheets. Other people marvel at Simons, whose grace under fire is complemented by their perfectly matched belts, shoes, and handbags.

Yeah, Simons' shit *seems* to be together...but under the surface, maybe it's not.

We all know plenty of Alvins and Theodores. They're not hard to spot—arriving fifteen minutes late to the meeting or calling frantically five minutes after that, because they just realized they have no idea where the meeting is to begin with.

Simons are harder. They've perfected the *illusion* of having their shit together, operating

Shit Simons may need help getting together

Prioritizing
Setting boundaries
Ending a relationship
Switching careers
Maintaining their sanity

under the mistaken belief that **being in demand, booked up, and perennially under the gun** equals "winning." They masquerade as busy little bees and perfectly productive overachievers — but their shit is on struggle mode even if you can't see it.

I know this because I used to know one particular Simon very well:

Me.

I lost my shit so you don't have to

In the past, I had my shit so outwardly together that nobody could see, let alone imagine, the turmoil happening inside my brain and body. I was so overcommitted that my day-to-day tasks were less like surgical strikes and more like ER triage. So yeah, I had it together in the sense that if you presented me with a problem, I could solve it. A project, I could complete it. A thorny philosophical question about the state of your romantic relationship, I could opine convincingly on it. I was a daughter, friend, student, employee, boss, wife, editor, cheerleader, psychologist, sounding board, and all-around **Get Shit Done Ninja.**

But seven or eight years ago, I was presented with a problem I didn't know how to solve.

I'd been unwell for most of the week. My stomach hurt. I had a low-grade headache. I couldn't seem to take in a deep breath and periodically wondered if it was my new bra causing the problem. (Spoiler alert: it wasn't.) As I was getting ready for work one day, I told my husband I was feeling nauseous.

"Maybe you're hung over?" he said.

While this hypothesis was not without merit in my early thirties (and, okay, even now in my late thirties), I was pretty sure that wasn't the cause of the tropical storm currently brewing somewhere in my torso.

In retrospect, I probably should have called in sick to work; it was a "Summer Friday," so we only had to show up for a half day and most people, including my boss, were on vacation. Also: I was actually sick. But Simon had shit to do! So Simon got on the train.

My disdain for the New York City subway is considerable (and well documented), and was greatly magnified by what happened that morning — which was me feeling like I was going to vomit for fifteen gruelling stops until I burst out of the train car at Fifty-Ninth Street and sort of rush-hobbled my way into the office so I could puke in peace. Or at least not in a trash can on the subway platform.

So there I was, hanging my head over the toilet in the twelfth-floor ladies' room at a major publishing house and...nothing. Apparently the storm was still gathering strength off the coastline. I went to my desk, fired up my computer, and emailed my husband *Ugh, still feel awful.* Then another wave came and I rush-hobbled down the hall to the restroom. Again: nothing.

Oh holy fuck, am I pregnant?

Back in my swivel chair, I tried to get comfortable so I could tackle the work I'd come in to do that day. After all,

I had my shit together! I was a mover and shaker, a can-do gal. Triumph-in-the-face-of-adversity was kind of my thing.

But then my arms started to go numb. This was new. Now I *really* couldn't breathe. I stood up and my vision blurred.

Have I been... poisoned? This was where my brain took me next. I shit you not. POISONED! OBVIOUSLY!

I staggered out of my office, leaned into a friend's cubicle, and said, "Call my husband, please. There is something seriously wrong with me." She wisely called the on-site nurse first. Then some security guards came to retrieve me in a wheelchair because I couldn't walk, and they wheeled me down to the nurse's office, where — and I'll spare you the next, like, three hours of this story — I was told that no, I was not pregnant or poisoned, but I'd probably had a panic attack.

Seriously? I thought. *This is the shit I have to deal with now? Panic attacks?*

Again, sparing you the long and winding road from panic attack *numero uno* to quitting my corporate job, giving fewer fucks, writing my first book, and then writing the book you are holding in your hands, the lesson I learned was: **Just because you are doing a ton of shit all day, every day, does NOT mean you have your shit together.**

It means you are a high-functioning human to-do list potentially on the verge of total mental and physical collapse. A Simon, if you will.

So gather round, my little chipmunks, and hear me when I say:

- Getting your shit together does **not** mean packing your calendar to the brim just for the sake of packing your calendar to the brim.

- It does **not** mean sucking it up, doing everything on your to-do list, then doing everything on someone else's to-do list, and doing it yesterday.

- And it does **not** mean sacrificing your mental and physical health to the cause.

What it **does** mean — for me, and for every Alvin, Simon, and Theodore on the spectrum — is *managing* your calendar and to-do list in such a way that the shit that needs doing gets done, and it doesn't drive you crazy along the way.

I call this "winning at life."

Winning at life
(without being an insufferable prick)

Point of order: You do not have to be an innately competitive person in order to win at life. Sure, under certain circumstances it can be extremely satisfying to crush your enemies, see them driven before you, and hear the lamentations of their women. If you *are* into categorical demolition of opponents, we probably shouldn't play Monopoly together, though I respect your gangsta. But if you're not typically big on "winning" at the expense of others, that's A-OK too, my gentle dumpling.

In my book — and in the Game of Life — you're competing exclusively against yourself. Not other players, not even the computer. Just you, clearing a path toward victory by getting your shit together and getting out of your own damn way.

Winning is getting what *you* want out of *your* time on planet Earth, whatever that entails. It could be the house, job, car, partner, or hairstyle of your dreams. Winning happens when you translate dreams into action and your actions change your reality. It's living YOUR best life, not denying anyone else theirs, and/or being an insufferable prick on the order of one Mr. Carlos Irwin Estévez. That's my core philosophy, and I hope you'll run with it. Or walk, swim, or cartwheel — I'm not picky, and this is not a race.

Life is like an adult colouring book

Okay, now we're getting down to brass tacks. I'm going to show you **what the process of getting your shit together and winning at life actually looks like.**

For me, this has meant living in the tropics and working for myself. For you, it could mean getting a promotion, or just going a week without drowning in your own inbox. Maybe it's circumnavigating the globe in an origami kayak. I don't know your life. But the beauty of having your shit together is that anything is possible.

Getting it together takes three steps.

1. **Strategize:** Set a goal and make a plan to achieve that goal in a series of small, manageable chunks.

2. **Focus:** Set aside time to complete each chunk.

3. **Commit:** Do what you need to do to check off your chunks.

Here's what these steps looked like for me, in the wake of that *Oh shit* moment I mentioned earlier:

To achieve my GOAL of quitting my corporate job with all its corporate benefits, I needed some cash reserves. First, I put out feelers to my freelancer friends. After setting up shop, I asked, how long had it taken to book jobs, and then actually start getting *paid* on those jobs? Taking into account their answers and my own plans, I concluded that three months' worth of expenses—mortgage, insurance, phone bill, pizza fund, etc.—would tide me over while I got my new freelance business off the ground.

When I added up my monthlies and multiplied by three...well, it was a lot. Nest eggs usually are. So my STRATEGY was to amortize, which is a fancy word for **"break it into small, manageable chunks which are then spread over time."** I did the maths. Saving that money in two weeks would be impossible, but saving it over one year was eminently doable.

Next, I made a chart with 365 squares and hung it on my refrigerator. Each square represented a day of savings. Then every morning, for a whole year, I FOCUSED for just a couple of minutes: I fired up my banking app, transferred a set dollar amount from my checking to my savings account, and used a red marker to colour in a corresponding square on my chart.

Every day, a small COMMITMENT. It didn't even hurt my wallet, because I'd divided my overall goal into 365 mini-goals.

As time went by and I watched the sea of red advance across my fridge, I got more excited about what it represented: cold hard cash, yes, but also freedom from corporate bullshit (and eventually year-round sunshine and unlimited access to palm trees). And because I was calmly proceeding toward my goal in **small, manageable chunks,** I was able to take on even more things that I *wanted* to do along the way, without feeling overwhelmed.

For example, during the course of the job-quitting and freelance business-starting (and essentially as a direct result of having my shit together on those fronts), I got a deal to write *The Life-Changing Magic of Not Giving a Fuck*. Huzzah! But there was a catch: the book—all 40,000 words of it—would be due in the absurdly short span of one month.

You read that correctly. *One motherfucking month.* Eleven months less than it took me to save up all that money, eight months less than it takes to gestate a human being, and two months less than the trial period during which one can test a thousand-dollar Casper Mattress and return it for a refund if not fully satisfied.

Well, I wanted to write the book, I wanted to hit my deadline, and I did not want to drive myself (or my husband) crazy. So what did I do? I looked at the calendar and made another plan. I determined that I'd have to generate a certain number of words per day (factoring in the occasional day off because, hangovers); then I set aside some time each day, sat down, and, you know, did it.

Strategize, focus, commit.

That's what having your shit together looks like.

Same deal with building a house in and moving to the Caribbean. Yes, it took some sacrifices, but just like my Quit-My-Job Fund, those were spread over time. My husband and I **strategized** on what we could afford and how long it would take, **focused** on small parts of the whole (him applying for loans, me corresponding with the builder); and **committed**—financially and psychologically— to both the overarching goal and the smaller, easier mini-goals along the way.

In this way, **life is like an adult colouring book.** You simply work your way through each little section until the big picture materializes before you.

When the new house was ready, it was time to put our Brooklyn apartment on the market. When the apartment

Get your shit together

was sold, it was time to get rid of furniture. Then arrange movers. Then pack. Then wake up in paradise with the birds chirping and the palm trees swaying and *OH MY GOD IS THAT A GIANT SPIDER?!?*

But I digress.

Grab those coloured pencils, because you've earned yourself a fun little exercise to illustrate my point!

Your real and metaphorical keys, phone, and wallet

If you're still with me, congratulations, because shit is about to get REAL. I'm going to show you **three tools** for getting your shit together — and as I said, it may surprise you to learn that you already have them in your possession.

You see, I have a theory that "getting your shit together" — metaphorically speaking — is like keeping track of your keys, phone, and wallet. With each of these three little things, you can do a bigger thing, such as unlock your house or order Chinese food or buy a bus ticket. They are essential life accessories. So whenever somebody tells me they've lost one or more of these items, I always think, *Seriously, get your shit together.*

But in case you thought the air was getting a little too thin up here on my soapbox, let me tell you a story.

Picture it: A mall in southern New Hampshire, 1990. Two twelve-year-old girls, footloose and fancy-free, visions of Guess? Jeans and The Body Shop dancing in their pre-teen heads.

I'd been dropped off with my friend Emily and all of my birthday and Christmas spoils ready to spend. I didn't have a lot of money growing up, and with my birthday falling in December, the end of the year always felt like hitting the lottery. This was a Big Day. I had probably sixty dollars and a few gift cards stowed away in a hideous embroidered purse that sort of puckered at the top when you pulled its dangly strings. It was purple and black and yellow and turquoise and looked like the upholstery in a Santa Fe dentist's office. I don't know, it was the nineties, what can I say?

Anyway, I was in a dressing room at Express when I realized... I no longer had my hideous purse.

I proceeded to lose my shit.

I mean, first I had literally lost my shit, and now I was

figuratively losing it. My stomach fell like an elevator with its cables cut. I saw black spots at the edge of my vision and I remember not being able to speak for at least a minute. (Actually, now that I think about it—*that* was probably Baby's first panic attack.)

To her eternal credit, Emily took charge. The plan was to retrace our steps through the mall and hope to all that was good and holy that either we would find my bag—with its contents intact—or someone would eventually turn it in to the Lost & Found. Was there even a Lost & Found? I didn't know and I didn't want to have to find out.

We scoured that mall for a good forty-five minutes, hopping from the JCPenney entrance to the food court, to Claire's Boutique and the dreamcatcher kiosk, to the Yankee Candle shop with its discounted holiday votives, then over to the Gap, me getting more panicky by the minute. As I hyperventilated my way into Spencer Gifts—that beacon of whoopee cushions and raunchy coffee mugs—I spotted my purse sitting quietly on the floor. Right where I'd left it while sifting through the X-rated greeting card display.

Maybe my bag was so ugly nobody wanted it (or thought it could possibly contain anything of value).

Maybe its lurid colours blended into the swirly carpet pattern and nobody even saw it while it sat there for an hour. All I know is, I thanked my lucky stars and I never lost a purse again. Or a wallet or a set of keys, for that matter.*

You may be thinking *What does any of this have to do with anything? And what's a "mall"? Is that like Amazon for old people?*

Please bear with me for another page or two, Your Honour. I believe I have a very enlightening point to make about your real and metaphorical keys, phone, and wallet.

But first, some real talk.

There is no excuse not to keep track of your house keys. They are the KEYS to your HOUSE. Knowing where they are should be a priority on par with remembering to get dressed before leaving your house. If you've ever waited for a locksmith wearing nothing but a hand towel and a nervous smile, you know what I'm talking about.

Same with your phone. Unless you took a hot tub time machine back to 1993, you have a cellular device that controls the vast majority of your life: calendars, contacts,

---

* My phone got stolen once, but then it got *returned,* which, if that's not karma for having my shit together most of the damn time, I don't know what is.

emails, and that infernal Facebook Messenger app. I bet it was an expensive piece of equipment, too, so maybe you ought to be more careful with it than you would be with an old stick of gum. Only one of those things won't cost you $500 if it falls out of your pocket in the back of a cab.

Then there's your wallet. It contains not only cash, but your ATM, credit, and health insurance cards; driver's licence; maybe a work ID and gym membership; and (one hopes) a perfectly good condom. If you lose your wallet you will have to replace *all of the shit in it,* and somebody might get pregnant.

IT'S NOT WORTH IT.
GET YOUR SHIT TOGETHER.

And guess what? If you can manage to stay on top of those three little life management tools, you can use them to get your metaphorical shit together too.

Remember when I talked about **strategy, focus, and commitment?** That was no coincidence, Grasshopper.

- Your keys are the ability to **strategize** — they unlock the next steps.

- Your phone is the ability to **focus** — make those calls, mark that calendar.

- Your wallet represents **commitment** — this is when you put your real or metaphorical money where your mouth is, to follow through on your plan. (Just don't let yourself get overdrawn at the real or metaphorical bank.)

GYST THEORY

KEYS = STRATEGY
+   +
PHONE = FOCUS
+   +
WALLET = COMMITMENT

SHIT + TOGETHER

For what it's worth, I believe in you! I think you can keep track of your keys, phone, and wallet. You can learn to strategize; having a good strategy in place will enable you to focus; and mastering those skills will make it easier to finally commit to your goals.

Why do I have such blind faith in a person I've probably never met? Because humans invented fire, mapped the Arctic Circle, and created hologram Tupac. We didn't do any of that shit without a plan! You're a born strategizer; you just need to dust off the natural ability that's been hiding under all your mental clutter. It's far more valuable than the old chamber pot your aunt Sharon took on *Antiques Roadshow,* and they gave her like four hundred bucks for that.

Let's talk strategy

As mentioned, strategy is **"a plan of action designed to achieve a goal."** So if your strategy has thus far been to throw up your hands like a helpless infant even though you are in fact a grown-up adult, then as Paul Simon might say, you might need to make a new plan, Stan.

From the time you were in shorts and pigtails — and whether you identify as an Alvin, Simon, or Theodore — you observed the cut-throat nature of swingball, lunch lines, and Spin the Bottle. You watched people jockey for position and you observed and internalized the outcomes. Maybe you succeeded, maybe you failed, maybe you never joined the fray — but I'm sure you at least recognized the *concept* of putting yourself in a strategic spot from which to vanquish all comers, nab the last bag of Doritos, or kiss your secret crush while looking all nonchalant about it.

Today, you've taken the bold step of admitting you want to win at life, not just swingball. The Game of Life has several levels — among them work, finances, relationships, and mental and physical health. I don't know which of these is giving you agita at the moment, but I do know that they can all be approached — and conquered — with the same combination of **strategy, focus, and commitment**.

Keys, phone, wallet.

For example, let's say you hate your job. Therefore, *get a new job* is the easiest goal in the world to set. Goal-setting is not rocket science. (Or tiny-ship-in-a-bottle-making, for that matter. How do they DO that?) But as you know, jobs themselves do not grow on trees. They don't walk up to you in the street like a stray dog and beg to be taken home. You can't get a job by swiping right all day on Tinder. (Though come to think of it, you can probably get another kind of job.)

No, to get yourself a new gig you have to apply and interview and before that you have to research places you might want to work or contact a headhunter and before that you probably have to polish your CV and before that — WHOA, SETTLE DOWN THERE, BUDDY, THIS IS ALL TOO MUCH FOR ME. I'M OVERWHELMED!

Yeah, I know. That's why you need a **strategy**. Calm down.

The good thing about a strategy, or a plan, is that it's **individually tailored to YOU and YOUR GOAL**. You know what your skill set is. You know how much time you have this weekend to work on your CV. You know how many days, weeks, or months you can survive under the conditions of your current job. All of this knowledge is like a big old ring of keys in your pocket or your purse or dangling from your belt like a medieval dungeon guard. (Which, by the way, is not a good look for anybody. Just sayin'.)

So which key unlocks which door?

Well, the one for "my skill set" unlocks the "other jobs I might be qualified for" door.

The one for "how much time I have this weekend" unlocks the "working on my CV" door.

And the one for "how long can I keep showing up at my current job without dying inside" unlocks the "when I look at it that way, I better get my shit together" door.

A strategy is simply all the small, manageable steps of a plan — your plan — neatly bundled on the key ring and ready to be put into action.

Focus pocus

In the twenty-first century, phones are basically magic. They do everything from making calls to taking pictures to spying on your nanny while you're at work. With this one little device, you can manage your entire life — work, dating, travel, banking — you name it, and there's an app for that. But although you may have twenty-five apps running in the background and a monster to-do list, **you can only** *use* **your phone to do one thing at a time.** Skype with your parents. Reply to your boss's email. Book a flight. Lay down the greatest Instagram caption EVER.

And much has been written by more science-y people than me about the **myth of multitasking,** but suffice it to say, it's not actually possible to do more than one thing at a time in general, not just on your phone. (With the exception of listening to music; although if you're trying to accomplish anything else while listening to *Purple Rain,* you don't deserve to be listening to *Purple Rain.*) The point being: If you think you're watching your daughter's football game *and* composing a clever rejoinder to your office nemesis, then you're doing at least one of these things badly, probably both.

The same goes for getting your shit together.

FOCUS. Small, manageable chunks. One at a time.

Back to the imaginary job hunt. You've identified your goal (get a new job) and laid out your strategy (step 1 of which is "update CV"). So grab your real or metaphorical phone and **schedule that step.** Set aside an hour on Saturday for CV updating. Do not go out for donuts, do not click on the *Daily Mail's* sidebar of shame or check the tennis scores.

You can be all *But I'm the Queen of Multitasking!* and I'll be all *Oh really? How's that been working out for you so far?*

Don't be a hero. **Give yourself the time and space to do the shit that needs doing, to get you closer to your goal.** If it's polishing your CV, give yourself an hour; if it's shopping for a new interview outfit, take an afternoon; if it's realizing that you have the wrong skill set and have to get an advanced degree to qualify for a different/better job, well then, that's where your focus needs to be for the next two to four years. In the end it'll be worth it. (And if your different/better job is as a Beyoncé impersonator, that's a smart career move. Bey may be all-seeing and all-knowing, but she doesn't do birthday parties in Jersey.)

Some of this may sound a touch facile at first—like, what if you really don't believe you have a few hours to spare, ever, for anything? I get it. I'm sure, for example, that there are an awful lot of working parents (and non-working parents, and working non-parents) ready to shut this book, hunt me down, and slap me with it right about now. But I promise I'll address that issue in part II, when we start getting jiggy with priority and time management.

For now, all you need to know is that once you've identified the strategy and narrowed your focus, **you're ready to commit.**

Saying "I do."

If you want to get a new job (or throw a killer dinner party, run a five-minute mile, clean your house, or write a novel, for that matter), you have to take each individual step that gets you there. You must put one real or metaphorical foot in front of the other. I liken this to taking out your real or metaphorical wallet and putting your real or metaphorical money where your mouth is. **Remember: It's not only dollars that can represent action and commitment.**

So if you've set a goal to get a new job and the first step in your strategy is polishing your CV, and you've put aside an hour on Saturday to focus on that and only that task — now you have to do it. **Get in the zone.** Sit down, open the document, and DO THE WORK. You set aside an hour, so use it.

Finally, it's important to note that **you're only as good as the last step you took.** Great work updating that CV! But if

Ways to get in the zone

Don your lucky underpants
Do five star jumps
Listen to the *Karate Kid*
    theme song
Light a scented candle
Pinch your cheeks to get
    that healthy glow

it sits in a folder on your computer gathering cyber-dust and you never send it out to potential employers, then your shit is not officially "together." You're more like Ross and Rachel when they were on a break, and we all know how that turned out.

You have to **commit *all the way.*** Shit or get off the pot, so to speak.

Of course, some people are all excuses and no action. They aren't overwhelmed or overbooked; they're just lazy, and they do the same thing, i.e., *nothing,* over and over again, expecting different results. Some of them are all up in my Twitter feed like *I don't give a fuuuuuuuuck about get- ting my shit together!* Haha, guys. I see what you did there. Read my first book, didja?

Yeah, I know. Stop giving so many fucks? That sounds awesome! Get your shit together? Boo, THAT SOUNDS LIKE TOO MUCH WORK.

Well, no shit, Sherlock. This is mental decluttering, not mental napping.

If you're a chronic bullshitter with no real goals in life and no intention of setting any, that's cool, but you just wasted £12.99.

"But [thing I want to do] is too hard!"

Saddle up, cowboy, because I don't believe in "too hard." If you're going to argue with me on this you should probably stop reading now and go see if your bookshop will refund your money. Or is it too hard to put on some pants, get in your car, drive to the store, and admit to the cashier that you don't actually want to get your shit together?

I thought so.

As far as I'm concerned, there are only **degrees of difficulty along an achievable continuum of goals.** If you set a realistic goal whose parameters are within your control, it can be achieved. I'm not going to go down the "But what if my goal is to be President even though I have zero qualifications" rabbit hole. Please don't be pedantic.

For example, I think it would be "hard" to run a marathon, whereas I have several friends who seem to find completing a 26.2-mile road race easier than being on time for a dinner reservation. Yet people all over the world manage both of these tasks every day, so neither can be "too hard," whereas only one person every four years gets elected President. Ergo, I wouldn't set the marathon-running goal for myself, but if I did, it would theoretically be achievable.

In other words, "hard" is subjective, but **"too hard" is just another way of saying "I quit before I even tried."** How about you sack up and keep reading?

And what do the rest of us say to those people?
Seriously, get your shit together!

The Power of Negative Thinking

As described in *The Life-Changing Magic of Not Giving a Fuck,* my patented **NotSorry Method** for mental decluttering gets rid of things that annoy you (fucks you don't want to give) to leave room for things that bring you joy (fucks you do want to give). Two steps. Very simple. Look into it.

For our purposes now, though, all you need to know is that the key to NotSorry is **focusing on the "annoy."** It's fun to cross things like *Formula One* and *company holiday parties* off your FUCKS I MAY OR MAY NOT GIVE list with a big black marker. (No joke, if you haven't read the book, this is exactly what it tells you to do.) Anyway, the same concept works for getting your shit together.

Allow me to explain.

There are many gurus out there for whom the word *aspirational* is a real turn-on. They want you to be the best version of yourself, work the hardest, and reap the most reward. And that's all fine and dandy (I'm looking at you, *Lean in 15* guy), but as I discovered when I started getting fan mail, a lot of people **aspire to have and to do *less*, not more.**

Which is why this anti-guru believes in **The Power of Negative Thinking.**

This is when, instead of daydreaming about *a theoretical future* of being richer, thinner, or tidier, you focus on NOT being broke, fat, and messy *in the here and now.* Turns out goal-setting **doesn't have to be about aspiring to what you want to be, so much as putting an end to what you *don't* want to be.** Channelling rage at the things that annoy you is a great motivational tool for getting your shit together! Well, maybe not "rage," per se, but displeasure. Discomfort. Unhappiness.

It sure worked for me.

I told you a bit about my Big Life Changes — going from New York City corporate ladder-climber to sipping-frozen-drinks-on-the-beach freelancer. Astute readers will recall that in the introduction, I specifically said **I was very unhappy** before making those changes.

Recognizing and wanting to eradicate that unhappy

feeling was what prompted me to get my shit together and set my first goal(s):

- To NOT be unhappy

- To NOT be employed by a corporation

- And to NOT suffer through another winter like those puppies in the RSPCA Christmas campaign

It may seem counterintuitive, but **until I focused on the negative, I couldn't find my way toward the positive.** The thing was, I didn't really know what happiness was going to look like for me; I just knew I didn't have it. I had no idea what freelance life or moving to a foreign country would entail, but I knew that staying in the frozen Northeast for another winter would *definitely* make me miserable. What I had was a highly recognizable, constant state of unhappiness (and low core temperature), so the only goal I could really wrap my head around was to make it stop.

It was less aspirational and more GET ME OUT OF THIS NOW I CAN'T TAKE IT ANY MORE. An *Oh shit* moment for the ages.

And once I set a goal to **eliminate the annoy**—then

strategized, focused, and committed to it—**the joy revealed itself**, bit by bit. Huh. Imagine that. (These days sometimes my only goal is to even out my tan lines, but that still takes strategy, focus, and commitment.)

So if you're unhappy living in debt, carrying twenty extra pounds, and/or using the backseat of your car as a mobile laundry basket—if it makes you sad or frustrated or angry to live this way—I say, **harness the Power of Negative Thinking and channel your feelings into action.** Rather than chasing those pretty, aspirational butterflies that have long seemed to hover just out of reach, stomp a few unsightly cockroaches that are right there on the floor in front of you.

That'll get your blood pumping.

Ready, set, goal!

But before you turn on the lights and scatter the roaches, there's one more mini-step in between. Take a minute to sit in the calm, bug-free darkness and ruminate on what constitutes winning at life. YOUR life.

What goals and results—be they material or emotional—

would see you doing a victory lap like [a much, much slower and less spectacularly chiselled] Usain Bolt? I'm not talking about what anyone else considers winning, or what goals and results you think you *should* want. Just the things that would make you happy.

Is it getting a new job, or just being less irritated at the one you have?

Is it improving your relationship with your significant other, or just ending things once and for all? (Related: Do you want to sleep on the couch tonight?)

Is it losing twenty pounds, or do you just feel *pressured* to go down a size? If it's the latter, please stop giving a fuck about the numbers — you're only adding to your mental clutter. If it's the former, we'll get your shit together and make it happen.

Well, *you'll* get your shit together. I'll just show you how.

11

SMALL SHIT:
Nailing down the day-to-day to build a better future

As you know by now, one of my favourite pastimes is "breaking things up into small, manageable chunks." So to keep things ultra-manageable for you (especially you, Theodore), we're going to start off easy—with the small shit. **Stuff you have to deal with on a regular basis,** like **being on time** and **not getting distracted** and **staying on top of your email.** Once you nail that down, life becomes infinitely easier and more pleasant. Then you can move on to the bigger stuff, like retirement planning or building a life-sized replica of Castle Grayskull on your lawn, if that's your jam.

Part II covers **where to begin,** tips for **time management,** how to **prioritize by procrastinating,** and the **difference between a "to-do" list and a "must-do" list.**

We'll also **wrangle your inbox,** have a heart-to-heart about **impulse control,** and go step by step through scenarios like **getting stuck late at work** and **spending beyond your means.**

Perhaps you're an Alvin or a Simon and you think you have these things covered, in which case you're ahead of the game. Well played! However, I humbly suggest that a refresher course could be just the ticket. (Also, there are some jokes that run through the whole book and you won't get them if you skip this part.)

In parts III and IV, we'll **expand into tougher shit** (such as the aforementioned retirement planning, as well as other fun aspects of being an adult), and dig into **deeper shit,** like mental health, existential crises, and those Big Life Changes I've been nattering on about.

For now, though, onward, to the small shit!

Beginning for beginners

What holds people back the most from getting their shit together? If you're a classic Theodore (or, say, an Alvin with Theodore rising), the answer is probably **"I don't even know where to begin."** It therefore makes perfect sense to begin the process of getting your shit together by...demolishing this lame excuse.

I'm sorry, but it *is* lame. This is the tough love portion of our journey—you'll thank me for it later. The fact is, every Alvin, Simon, and Theodore reading this book already knows the answer to "Where do I begin?" I know you know it because I told you way back on page 30.

You begin by **setting a goal.**

THE WHAT/WHY METHOD FOR SETTING GOALS

STEP 1:
WHAT'S WRONG WITH MY LIFE?

STEP 2:
WHY?

Once you ask yourself these two questions, you'll be on your way to a goal in no time.

The answer to step 1 (What's wrong with my life?) can be general, but not *ridiculously* so. For example:

"I'm broke" is something you can work with.

"Everything" is not a productive answer. You need to break that shit into small, manageable chunks.

"I'm in an unhealthy relationship with ennui" is a crock of shit and you know it.

So let's say you are in fact broke. The answer to step 2 (Why?) could be anything, such as:

I lost my job

I lost a bet

I devoted my last two paychecks to a Harley, realized I have nowhere to keep a motorbike, and now I'm renting a $69/month storage unit in perpetuity to house my midlife crisis toy.

Your goal has to *solve the problems* set forth by steps 1 and 2. Like so:

Get a new job (see page 42 for tips!)

Stop playing fast and loose with 200-to-1 odds

Sell motorbike, get rid of storage unit, find a cheaper way to have a midlife crisis.

Make sense? Here's another example, just off the top of my head:

What's wrong with my life? I'm way behind at work.

Why? I waste too much time dicking around online instead of doing things that are higher-priority.

Goal: Limit the amount of time I spend online.

If you happen to have the same sample answer for step 1 above, *your* answer to step 2 could be something different, like: "I say yes to too many lunch meetings that run over-long" or "I have a colleague who's always in my office bitching about her life." And your goal would address those reasons. Brown-bag it. Hang a kicky little DO NOT DISTURB ME, SHEILA sign on your door.

If your answer to step 2 is manifold (entirely possible; the workplace is a time-suck of epic proportions), write down several answers and set a goal for each of them. When it comes time to carry out those goals, you'll want to **prioritize, and start with the most important one** — a skill we'll be honing in due course.

Okay, one more for the road. I plucked this "What's wrong with my life?" scenario directly from the 2,400 results of my anonymous Get Your Shit Together Survey, which I'll reference periodically throughout the book.*

What's wrong with my life? The giant box for the TV that I bought eight months ago is still in the living room, leaning against the wall like it belongs there.

---

* It's no eight-year, double-blind, longitudinal study — as my editor was quick to point out — but it has provided valuable insight into people's common problems, aspirations, and complaints, plus a *soupçon* of unintentional comedy.

Why? Because I haven't taken it to the street.

Goal: Take the fucking box to the street.

(I hope whoever sent me that response is reading. They clearly need this method in their life.)

Now you try:

What's wrong with my life? _____

Why? _____

Goal: _____

There, you've begun. I told you it was easy.

The bar is too damn high

Holding yourself up to an *unreasonable* standard is no way to win at life. **It's okay to lower the bar a tad,** especially when you're just starting out. For example, normal people who want to lose weight aren't likely to wind up looking like Kate fucking Upton. Striving for that goal is like running toward a finish line that will always be moving farther and farther away, which is really discouraging. Why would you keep running if you knew the race would never end? You might as well give up now, go home, sit on the couch, and commune with a Costco-sized pallet of bite-size Mini Oreos. Which is probably what you've done — at least metaphorically speaking — and why you're reading this book. (Classic Theodore manoeuvre, BTW.)

Instead, **set realistic goals** based on what annoys you about *your* life, not based on someone else's measurements, and begin the process of sweeping it out the damn door. I meant it when I said mental decluttering was a solo mission. Leave Kate Upton out of it.

Time flies when you don't have your shit together

Once you know where to begin, it's time to think about *when*. You can set your clock by Theodores forgetting to set their clocks, but time management can also be the Achilles heel of the most competent Simons among us. Why is that? I mean, we're surrounded by time-telling devices in our homes, cars, offices, and everywhere else. Watches, iPhones, cable boxes, microwaves, Big Ben, sundials, THE SUN ITSELF.

These are built-in tools to help human beings manage time. Everyone should be using them!

But for people who don't have their shit together, **there never seems to be *enough* time.** Too much on the to-do list, too few hours in the day. If their life was a one-hit wonder, the chorus would be **"I don't know, I'm just really bad at time management."** Again, I'm forced to demolish some lame excuses here. Time is both infinite (until a giant asteroid wipes out Earth) and finite, in that there are only twenty-four hours in any given day and they must be used wisely.

Time, like irritable bowel syndrome, can be managed.

It's on the calendar

I want to take a twenty-second time-out here to discuss calendars and why you should own and learn to operate one. Calendars are more than kitschy laminated wall hangings or little cubes of scrap paper bearing funny quotes from *Seinfeld*. They are tools for winning at life. Not using a calendar is like playing Snakes and Ladders with no ladders. The only people who do not need calendars are drifters and deities. The former don't have anywhere to be and the latter are omnipresent. You? You need a calendar.

I happen to be a chronically early person. I hate to keep people waiting, and that's motivation enough for me. But I also know I'm lucky to have a healthy relationship with time. Time and I are copacetic. We understand each other — and **understanding time is key to getting your shit together.**

So why can't some people reach that understanding?

Well, after careful and completely unscientific observation of friends who have "poor time management skills," I came to realize that they share a common trait — and it's not that they enjoy keeping me waiting or they don't own a clock. It's that **they don't actually know how long it takes to do anything.**

One of them will text me *Jumping in shower. See you in 15,* even though she has never taken a fifteen-minute shower in her entire life. Her intentions are not malicious; some people just have no fucking clue how long it takes them to shower and get ready to leave the house. Fifteen minutes seems about right, sure, and while you're at it — *Headed to the Post Office, see you in 5!*

Uh-huh.

Therefore, if you are one of these people [waves to an old roommate], and **if you hate being late as much as I**

hate the New York motherfucking Yankees, you can do something about it.

(And if you don't hate being late, then I guess you must love composing that charming song-and-dance routine you put on every time you have to explain your tardiness to colleagues and dinner companions. How does it go again? *Something-something-traffic-something-couldn't-find-my-something-got-stuck-on-the-phone-with-oh-my-God-you-wouldn't-believe-something-something* . . . You realize you're not fooling anyone, right?)

Well, if and when you're ready to be reliable and courteous rather than late and completely full of shit, the first step in improving your time management skills/getting your shit together is to **time yourself doing daily tasks.**

For example, before you get in the shower, set the stopwatch app on your phone (or one of those portable plastic kitchen timers, which can easily be repatriated to the bathroom), and keep it running until you're actually finished getting ready. Do this every day for a week and then crunch the numbers. Had to shave on Tuesday? Ten extra minutes. Took a whore's bath on Friday, minus five. When you're staring at your times and forced to confront reality, you'll have no more excuses to—as George W. Bush might say — misunderestimate the time it takes to perform your morning ablutions.

TASK: _____

DAY	TIME	NOTES
Sunday	_____	_____
Monday	_____	_____
Tuesday	_____	_____
Wednesday	_____	_____
Thursday	_____	_____
Friday	_____	_____
Saturday	_____	_____

The same could go for leaving work. Whether you have to get to the airport or meet someone for dinner (or relieve the nanny, or pick up dry cleaning before the shop closes, or any of a million things one might have to do after work), people with poor time management skills usually *severely* misunderestimate how long it takes to finish up the workday. And I'm only talking about getting out of the office — not even travelling *from* the office *to* the airport or the restaurant. Simply extricating yourself from the building can take a lot longer than you might think.

If this sounds familiar, you could try spending a week exploring this particular Twilight Zone.

For one day, resolve to neither gab with anyone nor use the bathroom on your way out. Time yourself from the moment you punch out or turn off your computer (or power down the fro-yo machine, or whatever) until you *Exit Stage Left*.

THAT'S how long it takes to "leave work." **You have your baseline.** Next, you need to factor in the variables.

For the rest of the week, just press a button on your watch or phone when you stand up to leave, and don't touch it again until you're out the door, no matter what happens. If you get waylaid by a coworker or a sudden downward urge (which better include two minutes for washing your hands, mister), record the results, then average them in with your baseline time. This is the easiest homework in the world, and it will give you a much more accurate sense of where you stand when it comes to *Leaving the office. See you in 10!*

And when you feel like you have an accurate sense, **there's no harm in padding that shit.** You can always circle the block so you're not ringing your friend's doorbell ten minutes before the dinner party starts, but at least you won't be slinking into your seat like a grade-A tool in the middle of her heartfelt toast. Bad chipmunk!

But please note: I'm not asking you to shower faster, kick your kids out of the house without breakfast, or jack your beanstalk without finishing. **The secret to time management isn't speeding up or slowing down.**

> ## Other shit you could time yourself doing
>
> Commuting (or getting from any point A to any point B)
> Working out
> Balancing the books
> Getting your kids out the door for school
> Reading the paper cover to cover
> Masturbating

It's about **strategy** and **focus**. (Strategy: Y = how much time does X take? Focus: if X is a necessary task, schedule Y minutes/hours to get it done; and/or undertake X task only when you *have* Y minutes/hours available.) In other words, don't try to shove a square phone call with your mother into a round five minutes.

Once you understand **how time applies to your life,** you'll be able to use it as a force for good instead of a force for missing flights or pissing off your dinner date. Meanwhile, perhaps invest in a sundial, which is a perfect visual reminder to keep working on your time management skills. And they're quite pretty.

Your best friend and worst enemy

Time is the mother ship from which two competing forces — **prioritization and procrastination** — descend to create order or wreak chaos in your life.

These mental houseguests rear their heads around every corner, especially in the top three problem areas revealed by my survey: **Work** (i.e., email/correspondence/ project management), **Finances** (i.e., time as it relates to saving $), and **Health** (i.e., scheduling fitness and/or relaxation so you can win at life without *also* losing your mind).

Each is integral to taming your to-do list — a thing many people need serious help doing. Even I need help doing that sometimes. Which is why when I feel myself starting to slip into **Fuck Overload**™, I get my shit together and prioritize.

Best Friends 4-EVA

Prioritization is BFFs with strategy. You want to get in on that action, because when it comes to a to-do list, writing one down is only half the battle. Next, you have to **whittle it down,** according to what you need to do first and what can be pushed off until later.

Fuck Overload™

Giving too many fucks—without enough time, energy, or money to devote to them—keeps you overbooked, overwhelmed, and overdrawn. This leads straight to Fuck Overload™, a state of anxiety, panic, and despair. Possibly tears. Despair, for sure. Why? Because even if you really need to give all of those fucks, **you cannot give them all at once.** That's where prioritizing comes in handy. And if you *don't* really need to give all of those fucks, well, I know a book that can help.

I use a running to-do list as a catch-all for everything I know I have to do in the near future—basically whenever I realize I have to do something, I write that shit down. I'm always adding to my list ("update credit card auto-pay" or "order penis-stemmed martini glasses for hen party"). Once I put a task in writing, I feel better equipped to enjoy my three nightly glasses of wine without worrying that I'll forget what I needed to do this week.

Then, each morning after regretting that third glass

of wine, I consider the amount of time I actually have in which to complete each task (credit card payment is due tomorrow, hen party is in three weeks). This tells me **which ones take priority,** so I can reorder my list from most to least urgent.

Finally, I look at my prioritized items and determine what truly, madly, deeply has to get done TODAY, and I move those things to a fresh piece of paper. This is the process by which you **turn your to-do list into a must-do list.** (I see you rolling your eyes, but who's the anti-guru here? It wouldn't kill you to take notes.)

Today, my running to-do list looks like this:

- Touch up my roots

- Do laundry

- Write 500 words

- Watch the Red Sox game

- Pick up prescription

- Order birthday gift for husband

The prioritized version of the list looks like this:

- Pick up prescription (I need to start taking it ASAP)

- Write 500 words (daily word count necessary to keep deadline achievable)

- Touch up my roots (eh, I can go another day without)

- Do laundry (I need those pants two days from now)

- Order gift for husband (whose birthday is in two weeks)

- Watch the Red Sox game (there are 72 games left in the season)

And my **must-do** list looks like this:

- Pick up prescription

- Write 500 words

When I pare my list down to the truly necessary tasks, those are the only two things I really need to get done *today*. The rest of it is not "must-do." (My savings plan is already so ingrained in me that I do it without putting it on the list, but I've been at this longer than you have.)

Now my **day looks much more approachable.** I feel less panicky about getting everything done, because there are not that many things. I know exactly where I have to start, and to top it all off, I realize I now have more time than I thought I did (back when I was in the throes of Fuck Overload™) to tackle a few other, less urgent things.

I can do laundry *while* I'm writing. I can skip the gift-ordering because I'm not sure what I want to get him yet anyway and I have a couple of weeks to sort it out. And if I get my work and my laundry done before 7:00 PM, I can settle in for the David Ortiz farewell tour with a clear conscience and a bottle of Pinot Noir. I sure do love me some Big Papi.

Tomorrow, "touch up my roots" migrates onto the must-do list but "pick up prescription" and "do laundry" have fallen off. Everything is still manageable. That's **the magic of prioritization.** Like playing the kazoo, it's really not that hard, it makes you feel good, and anyone can do it.

THE MUST-DO METHOD

1. MAKE A TO-DO LIST.
2. PRIORITIZE ITEMS BASED ON URGENCY.
3. MOVE WHAT HAS TO GET DONE <u>TODAY</u> TO A MUST-DO LIST.
4. DO THAT STUFF AND SAVE THE REST FOR TOMORROW.
5. REPEAT STEPS 1-4.

Sleeping with the enemy

Here's where things get tricky, because your other mental houseguest—procrastination—is a fickle mistress. Procrastination can aid you in both postponing action *and* in doing less urgent or more pleasurable things in place of doing the truly urgent and/or unpleasant. Either way, giving in to it can send you into Fuck Overload™ faster than Alec Baldwin gets thrown off a plane for being an asshole.

You might get there if you postponed action all over the goddamn place — if you **mistakenly viewed ALL the items on your to-do list as "must-do,"** knew you couldn't possibly get them done, and became paralyzed by inaction. At this point, you called in sick. You RSVP'd regrets. You hid under the bed until the bad man went away.

(More real talk, my little chipmunks: Anyone who says the biggest reason they can't get anything done is because they have "too many things" on their to-do list, probably has too many things on said list because they keep postponing doing *any* of them, and the list just gets longer and longer.)

You also might get to Fuck Overload™ because **you did all of the low-priority things and none of the high-priority ones.** This self-deception will not serve you well over time. Like, if I spent all day out shopping for my husband's birthday gift but didn't do any writing, I might have tricked myself into thinking I got some shit done, but tomorrow morning I'd have double the word count to achieve and I'd be back under the bed like that girl from *Taken*. Uncool.

Or maybe **you did a bunch of things that weren't even on the list!** That's a real bait and switch right there. Clever chipmunk.

Actually, let's look at that one a little more closely. Humour me.

If you've ever been on a diet, you may be familiar with the idea of keeping a "food journal" of everything you put in your mouth, which is an age-old way to create awareness around your eating habits. It helps you realize how much snacking you do without thinking, how many times you reach for seconds, and how long you've been deluding yourself that there's only one serving in a fifteen-ounce "Party-size Bag" of Doritos.

So how about instead of a food journal, you start a **Procrastination Journal,** where you list all the things you find yourself doing this week to procrastinate the shit you *really* have to get done? I'll give you some space below, but if you need more room, by all means, staple a few extra sheets right in here. The longer your list, the more emphatically this whole point gets made, which is good for my brand.

*Things I did that weren't on my to-do list to
procrastinate doing things that were: a journal*

_____ _____ _____

_____ _____ _____

_____ _____ _____

_____ _____ _____

_____ _____ _____

In case you're wondering, I'm not immune to this behaviour myself; I just hide it well. In the spirit of solidarity, I give you:

*Ten things I've done that weren't on my to-do list to
procrastinate doing things that were*

1. Cut my cuticles

2. Researched various skin conditions I might have

3. Watched *Ocean's Eleven* for the fiftieth time

4. Engaged in fruitless political debate on Facebook

5. Folded someone else's laundry

6. Conducted a Tabasco vs. Crystal hot sauce blind taste test

7. Colour-coded my ChapStick collection

8. Tried (and failed) to memorize the lyrics to "Nuthin But a 'G' Thang"

9. Contemplated the divinity of Helen Mirren

10. Kegels

So now you're thinking *Fine, and ew, I didn't need to know about the Kegels, but for the love of God HOW do I stop procrastinating??? That's why I bought this book!*

I hear you. It's a huge problem. Doing nothing at all, or doing only the low-priority shit, doesn't help you in the long run. Until now, you haven't been able to get procrastination off your mental pull-out couch, and it's used up all your mental laundry detergent.

Well, I'm not going to tell you how to banish procrastination.

You've got to be fucking kidding me.

Hey, hey, no need to get testy. In fact, I'm about to

give you *exactly* what you bought this book for! Your friendly neighbourhood anti-guru has some WACKY IDEAS.

You know that old saying "Keep your friends close but your enemies closer"? Well, that's exactly how to deal with procrastination. If it's going to stick around rent-free, you have to make it work FOR you, not against you. You can use it to **postpone actions that are low-priority** in order to turn your overwhelming to-do list into a manageable must-do list. **Responsible procrastination, FTW.**

Pitting your mental houseguests against each other helps you recognize non-urgent tasks (prioritize), set them aside (procrastinate), AND focus on what you really **must do** (win at life). Maybe having roommates isn't so bad after all.

Get your shit together: a flowchart

Good news! Any time you're looking for a responsible way to procrastinate, you could do so by consulting this handy flowchart. It's simple and easy-to-follow, and even staring blankly at it is more productive than staring blankly at other things, such as walls or your cat.

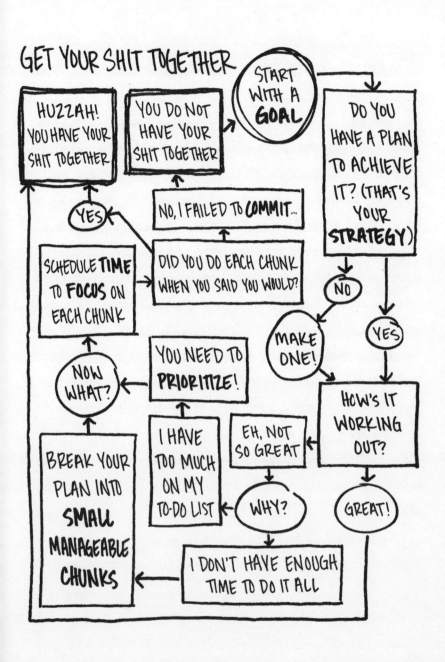

Where does the time go?

Earlier, I promised to address the **folks who don't believe they *have* any extra time**, because their days are already bursting at the seams with shit to do. I'm particularly sympathetic to this belief because I lived my life that way for thirty-plus years. **"There aren't enough hours in the day"** (or week, or month) was a mantra of sorts, and it felt very true when I was saying it to explain why I was sleeping in instead of working out or ordering pizza instead of cooking dinner.

But it wasn't totally true. What was true was that I **prioritized** sleeping over exercise, and convenience over some sort of Martha Stewart fantasy that I don't actually care to attain. It's not that I didn't have the hours in the day; it's that I didn't want to *use* them for calisthenics and cooking, and I've learned to recognize and admit that. #NotSorry

Unlike me, however, you may be a chipmunk with kids who require "vitamins" in their dinner. You may also be getting home too late at night to start any kind of meal (Martha-level or not) and have it on the table before those kids need to be off to bed. I'm not saying you're not busy, and I'm not saying you necessarily have the freedom to dial up a large pepperoni every time you don't feel like cooking.

What I *am* saying is that every single thing you have to do in any given day CAN be assigned a priority level, which will help you juggle it all. If you finally admit to yourself that you don't give a fuck about some of it, even better. But the rest is "need to do" and "want to do," which is what getting your shit together is all about.

Prioritizing takes you BEYOND the magic of not giving a fuck, into a land of ass-kicking and name-taking. Theodores will marvel at their new-found levels of productivity; Alvins will realize that life doesn't have to be such a slog; Simons will hone their natural capacity for efficiency and feel even more superior to their brothers than they already did.

Hypothetically, let's say you are a nine-to-fiver with two kids and a "not enough hours in the day" problem.

Dinner is a big part of that, so maybe the solution is to have meals on hand that either don't take much time to prepare, or are *already* prepared (by you, not Papa John). A few batches of freezable repasts concocted over the course of a weekend can be parcelled out on a nightly basis. Chilli. Burger patties. Lasagna. That kind of thing. A nice casserole never hurt anybody.

But let's *also* say that your weekends are stuffed to the brim. The kids are home from school so they need tending, or ferrying back and forth from whatever kids do these days. Gymnastics? I don't know; I spent my childhood reading in my bedroom, but that's neither here nor there. Perhaps gardening beckons. Then laundry. Then errands. You're starting to feel like standing over a hot oven for six hours is not conducive to all the other shit you have to do in your forty-eight-hour reprieve from the workweek.

You know what that feeling is? **Fuck Overload**™. You. Need. To. Prioritize.

Pick a time frame — e.g., today, this week, or this

weekend. What's on your to-do list for that time frame? What things are the most urgent? And what absolutely has to happen today (or this week, or this weekend)?

Then, **make your own version of the to-do and must-do lists from pages 72–73,** pertaining solely to your household tasks (not your job; that's a different part of the book, different set of lists). If you can't do it right now, take out that real or metaphorical phone, find yourself an hour to focus, and pencil it in. Otherwise you might never get to it and I will have written this entire book in vain, which is an extremely depressing thought.*

And don't try to be sneaky, Alvin. You can't double shit up together on one line (like "shop and cook"); you really have to assign each task **its own entry in the must-do hierarchy.** ("Grocery shopping" comes before "make lasagne" which comes before "do the dishes.")

Making these lists is **prioritizing *in action*.**

---

* Thanks in advance for keeping my spirits up. Much appreciated!

ALL THE SHIT I HAVE TO DO AROUND THE HOUSE

_____
_____
_____
_____
_____
_____
_____
_____

ALL THE SHIT I HAVE TO DO AROUND THE HOUSE, **IN ORDER OF URGENCY**

_____
_____
_____
_____
_____
_____
_____

ALL THE SHIT I **MUST** DO AROUND THE HOUSE

_____
_____
_____
_____
_____

If feeding your family takes top priority, what's next on your list? Grocery shopping, which you might be able to fit in while the kiddos are out swinging those plastic bats. Then carving out time to cook, which could be nightly (easy meals) or in batches (frozen delights). A slow cooker is your friend, friends. And let's see…the young'uns have to sort their own clothes before they're allowed to go out, laundry can be done while your lasagne's in the oven, and you know what? The grass can probably wait another week to get cut. Next weekend, it goes higher on the priority list and you cough up for a pizza.

And if you're a new parent with a baby, there may be no gymnastics practice, but there's a lot of other shit to deal with.* If you have a partner, you each get a list! If you don't, you may be prioritizing "find a babysitter" or "see what Grandma's up to this weekend."

(If you'll kindly put down your slappin' hand and just give it a *try*, you really might find it helpful.)

I can't account for every permutation of lifestyle and parenthood, but no matter what your situation is; how much help you do or don't have; and whether your kids

---

* Pun absolutely intended.

play sports or sit quietly in their rooms rapping with Laura Ingalls Wilder, my point is: **Once you have a handle on your priorities, you can schedule them in.**

And, guys? The more shit you have to do and the less time you think you have to do it, **the more you NEED the must-do list in your life.** It is in fact true that "there aren't enough hours in the day" to do everything. But you don't have to do everything.

You only have to do the things that you *prioritized*.

Frailty, thy name is distraction!

Like Arya Stark, distraction comes in many guises, and she is here to fuck your shit *up*.*

I'm not talking about legit last-minute "must-dos," but rather about an insidious venom that poisons your

---

* Those of you caught up on season six of *Game of Thrones* will get that reference. Those who aren't, I don't want you complaining that I spoiled it for you, so I left it vague. Those who don't even watch *Game of Thrones*, just trust in the metaphor, okay, guys?

best-laid plans from within. **If focus is akin to the phone on which you schedule your life, distraction is like losing said phone.** Your day is turned completely upside down. You're flailing around like a chicken with its SIM card cut off. Suddenly you feel compelled to drop everything, run to the nearest computer, and inform everyone you know *Lost my phone. If you need me, email!* (Which, if you think about it, is only adding to your level of distraction — I could get so much more done in a day if people would stop emailing me.) Nothing is getting accomplished until you have that device back in your hot little hand and your ability to focus is restored.

Therefore, much like you need to improve your relationship with time, you need to **distance yourself from distraction.**

There are three easy ways to do this:

Take evasive action.
Just like you know you should board up your house's windows before a hurricane, you know your own weaknesses. Don't let Arya exploit them! If you have a compulsive Twitter-checking problem

that eats into your productivity, don't keep the site/app open while you're trying to get shit done. Board it up and throw away the nail gun.

Stop, drop, and roll.

If, despite your best intentions, you find yourself coming out of a fugue state with Twitter open on your screen and you don't remember how you got there, treat the situation like you would if you were literally on fire. Stop scrolling, drop your hands to your sides, and roll away from your device long enough to snuff out the urge.

Pencil it in.

There's no harm in taking a mental break every once in a while. A break only becomes a dangerous distraction when it's unplanned or goes on way too long. (Fine, maybe not Arya Stark–level dangerous, but life isn't going to win itself, guys.) If you know you can't resist the lure of that little blue bird, just pad your overall notion of "how long it's going to take me to do X task" with an extra ten minutes of recharging, whatever that looks like for you—catching up with the latest on Rob and Blac Chyna, discovering your Hogwarts house, or clicking on through to see what @EmergencyKittens has to offer. Meow, that's more like it.

The Wizard of Impulse Control

Earlier in the book, you may have noticed that one of my off-the-cuff examples of not having your shit together included being "fat." As in: "if you're tired of being broke, fat, and messy." Please don't take that as an indictment from me about your pants size. Weight loss just happens to be something that comes up over and over again in relation to not having one's shit together, so it deserves to be addressed.

While I'm neither a dietician nor a personal trainer, as far as I can tell a diet or a workout regimen is just a **strategy** (weight loss/fitness goal + plan to achieve it), and sticking to your strategy requires **focus** (on individual meals and workouts) and **commitment** (eating the right stuff, moving the right body parts). The best diet book not on the market is only two pages long: EAT LESS. MOVE MORE.

Easy enough, right? You could be unstoppable! Except for one pesky problem: **impulse control.**

Impulse control should not be confused with distraction, which comes at you from all sides, when you least expect it, and in many forms. It's hard to fight distraction, because you can't control all of the *scenarios* in which it exists. That shit is sneaky. But impulses — to snack, to eat ice cream for breakfast, to stay snuggled in bed rather than sweating it out on the elliptical machine — those are all noted, processed, and acted upon (or not) by a single entity: you.

You haven't been "distracted" by a piece of cake. You've acted on an impulse to slather gooey buttercream frosting on your tongue that, in the moment, was stronger than your desire to weigh less or be more fit. And there is nothing inherently wrong with that. But if acting on that impulse contributes to your feelings of anger, sadness, or frustration — to falling short of your goals — then you may need to admit **you have a problem employee**

at the impulse control station, get your shit together, and confront him head-on.

If distraction is Arya Stark, then impulse control is more like the Wizard of Oz. This isn't some badass changeling assassin. Nope, just a man in a silly waistcoat pulling mental levers willy-nilly behind the curtain of your brain, causing trouble. He gets away with a lot when you refuse to look behind that curtain and reprimand him. Once you start paying attention, he'll have no choice but to fall in line.

Here are a few talking points to get you started:

> *Hey, Wizard, cut that shit out!*
>
> *I want to fit into the suit I bought for Greg's wedding, not eat that bag of peanut M&M's and then cry myself to sleep.*
>
> *I'm excited about the tennis arms I'm currently developing, and I'll thank you not to impede my progress to the gym this morning.*
>
> *How about you pull the lever for "Feelin' good about myself today" instead of the one for "Fuck, I did it again."*
>
> *I'm on to you, buddy.*

The Wizard of Impulse Control is nothing but a fraud in a silly waistcoat. You're in charge here, and you tell *him* what to do, not the other way around. And seriously, a fraud in a silly waistcoat? Is that really what's stopping you from going to the gym?

I thought not.

Making the sober decision

The hardest time to control your impulses is when you're intoxicated. Believe me, I've been there. I was wearing a traffic cone on my head and the Wizard just stood around taking pictures. What a dick.

This is why I've started making "the sober decision" — which curbs not only my drinking but also the side effects, such as inhaling large quantities of food two hours after I ate a perfectly good dinner. (I don't like to diet, but I also don't like having to buy new pants three times a year just because I can't, you know, control my impulses.)

Making the sober decision essentially means **giving the Wizard the night off**. There will be no in-the-moment, tequila-fuelled impulses to control, because I already controlled them *before I left the house*. For example, I decide — out loud and preferably in front of someone else who can remind me of it later — that I'll "only have three drinks" so I "don't order and consume an entire pizza after midnight." Then I'm forced to revisit my pledge when the bartender (or my friend Phil) tries to tempt me with round four.

This strategy is not 100 per cent effective, for obvious reasons, but it has helped me avoid a LOT of unpleasantness. It turns out that not only do I eat better when I'm neither shit-faced nor battling a hangover, there's also a strong correlation between having made the sober decision and not having thrown up, blacked out, or woken in a cold sweat concerned about emails the Wizard of Impulse Control may or may not have sent last night.

Correspondence course

Ah, you were wondering when we'd get to email, weren't you? It's a bitch, I know. In the modern era, staying on top of email is the embodiment of the old saying, "It's not easy, but somebody has to do it," and alas, that somebody is you. **And if you're constantly running behind, the time you spend typing could very well be to blame.**

(Not to mention time spent hunting for the perfect emoji. They have a wild boar, two dragons, and a puffer fish, but no Aladdin Sane? How often do *puffer fish* come up in people's text conversations? A lot less than David Bowie comes up in mine, I assure you.)

Anyway, for better or worse, keeping your shit together means managing the fuck out of your email — personal and professional — not to mention text messages, Slack channels*, Snapchat, Fumblr, FacePlace, MyLink, whatever. These forms of communication can be necessary, unnecessary, fun, or tedious, but they are ALL time-consuming, which is something a lot of people don't take into account when they blithely press Send on their thirty-seventh "Great, thanks!" of the day.

I'll be using email as a primary example because it's

---

* I hate Slack, the communication tool meant to "revolutionize email," with every fibre of my being. If you don't know what it is, consider yourself lucky.

the twenty-first century, but the same general principles apply to all correspondence, such as unearthing your bills, RSVP cards, and Habitat autumn sale vouchers (hey, 20 per cent off a sofa is nothing to sneeze at) from a year's worth of White Company catalogues that are useless to you unless you're ready to spend your entire annual clothing budget on a single cashmere jumper.

Where were we? Right, email.

Okay, so now, rather than cowering at your desk like, I don't know…a *coward,* I'm going to need you to sit up straight, flex those typing fingers, and get to work. If your inbox is Mount Everest, let's channel your inner Sherpa and get climbin'.

It's not the size of the inbox, it's how you use it

Pleading **"I get too much email"** as an excuse for not having your shit together is like saying "There are too many mosquitos in my garden so I'm going to just sit here and let them devour me whole rather than mist my body in readily available bug spray and light some citronella candles."

!!!NEWSFLASH!!! Most of us get a shitload of email. But it's not necessarily "too much" based on volume. It may just **seem** **like too much for** *you* **based on** *your* **current organizational systems,** which are either half-assed or non-existent.

Yes, some of us get more than others, but **quantity of email is not really the problem. Time management is the problem.** The reason you feel like you have too much email is because you are not *dealing with* your email in a timely, efficient fashion.

Apart from unsubscribing to mailing lists* and begging your father to take you off his dirty joke chain, there is almost nothing you can do to reduce the volume of email you receive. All you can do is attack it like Ed Norton attacks his own split personality, played by Brad Pitt, in *Fight Club*. (Sorry if I just ruined that movie for you, but you have emails to return before you can watch it anyway.)

But lest you get discouraged, notice that I said "almost" nothing you can do. There is one simple tactic you can employ to reduce the number of messages you get.

You can reduce the number that you *send*.

---

* Unroll.Me is the *shit*.

Reining in your sending habits

Do you treat your outbox as your own personal verbal vomitorium? Do you spend hours composing long, perfect emails that nobody ever reads? Or maybe you have eight different chains going with the same person, even though each one is about the same project (or the same Channing Tatum movie)?

Well, if part of your overflowing inbox problem is YOU, then you can cut that shit off at the source. Here are a few techniques to get you started on **sending fewer emails:**

That was not Tom Jones

You want to reach out and cyber-touch someone for fun or because you're bored (procrastinating much?) so you send three innocuous but unnecessary emails — about the weather, the sale at SpecSavers, and the guy who might have been but probably was not Tom Jones on the bus during your morning commute. You spend two minutes composing each email and — wonder of wonders — you receive three replies. Which you then spend two more minutes (each) reading, and possibly replying to (another two minutes). The **Constant Cycle of Reply** continues. Suddenly, you've spent twenty minutes in three different useless email conversations today, and you wonder why your inbox is swelling like a pregnant lady's ankles in August?

I have a ways to go on this front myself, but I try to be judicious. Sometimes I go so far as to type out the two-minute message, then think for a second about whether it's opening an annoying can of worms (for me, or for the person on the other end), and delete it. So maybe I lost two minutes and one second, but at least I saved myself time dealing with a potential reply, not to mention saved my husband a useless story about not-Tom-Jones.

Go all-inclusive

If you have a boss/coworker/client you email regularly, try to condense your communiqués into one or two messages instead of five, six, or sixteen. If your question or notion isn't time-sensitive, put it into a draft message that you add to all week and then send it all at once. This also helps you separate the wheat from the chaff — if you keep running drafts for your eyes only, then by Wednesday you might realize Monday's question was stupid. Delete it, and nobody else will ever have to know.

Do it the old-fashioned way

Pick up the phone. Journey across the hall. Fire up the walkie-talkies. You might spend less time having a single, live conversation with another human than you would going back and forth over email — especially if you're spending valuable time trying to get your "tone" right. Tone is a thing that comes across pretty fucking clearly right out of your mouth, no emoticons necessary.

Who cares?

Not every idea that pops into your head has to be committed to email and sent off immediately like a typhoid case to the quarantine tent. Before you start typing, ask yourself: *Does this even fucking matter?* Half the time, it doesn't.

And here are some techniques for **sending *better* emails.**

Just the facts, ma'am

Do you agonize over composing work emails, and then the people on the other end don't do half (or any) of what you asked for, and you have to follow up with them a week later anyway? That's because they saw your name in their inbox and their auto-response was "tl;dr."* Your emails are a thing of informative, emotionally nuanced beauty, but they are TOO FUCKING LONG. I've been on both ends of this equation (anti-gurus: they're just like us!) and it doesn't end well for anyone.† In act II, scene two of *Hamlet,* notorious windbag Polonius announces, "Brevity is the soul of wit." Well,

---

* "too long; didn't read"

† Dear Former Colleague: Hi, I know I need to send shorter, more concise emails — I'm working on it. But I also get real uppity when people who can't seem to do their jobs tell me it's *because* they "get too much email." We all need to take responsibility here, so maybe dial back on the *Project Runway* recaps with your BF and your inbox would get a little more manageable.

(And yes, that was directed at a very specific person. I'm not too proud to say I hold grudges like Lennie Small holds rabbits.)

it's the soul of effective email communication at work, too.

You: Stick to the important shit, no rhetorical curlicues, and spend less time composing your missive. They: Actually read it. Everyone: Wins.

Ask leading questions

Anytime you see a press conference on TV, there are about thirty journalists for every one who gets to ask a question of the celebrity, politician, or FBI director at the podium. That means if they get called on, their question has to count, and count big. One, maybe two sentences, delivered succinctly. Think of your emails the same way. Ask the thing you most need answered in the very first line, and you're much more likely to get an answer. Also, you may realize you don't need lines two through twenty-nine.

Start the clock

Establish urgency up front (not, however, with those red exclamation points — those are email suicide). Instead, use clear, informative language near the top of your message, such as "I need to know by 5 PM." Putting a time frame on someone's response may feel a little pushy at first, but as long as you're not the Intern Who Cried Wolf, people are likely to respond better to a specific deadline than to any kind of mealy-mouthed "When you have a moment."

If it's that low a priority, you probably shouldn't even be sending this email.

"Great, thanks!"

If you're a compulsive responder, you could save yourself a lot of time on those pernicious "Great, thanks!" emails that many people hate to receive anyway, because they crowd up the inbox. At five seconds per reply, to, say fifty emails a day, your time saved looks like this:

$$\text{4 minutes/day} \Rightarrow \text{5 days/week} = \text{20 minutes/week} \Rightarrow \text{18 HOURS/YEAR}$$

That's two and a quarter eight-hour workdays you could be using to get other shit done, or call in sick with "food poisoning" and take a long weekend at your friends' cottage in West Clare. Not that I would ever do such a thing, mind you.

But for the sake of argument, let's say you've got a pretty good handle on your own sending habits. Either you never had a problem to begin with (sure you didn't), or you've been taking the preceding advice to excellent results (you're welcome). And although you've successfully weaned your dad off sending you boob memes, the volume of *received* still has you snowed under, *Shining*-style.

What you need is a different horror-movie-as-antidote: *The Purge*. It might take longer than two hours to sit through, but by the end you'll have goose bumps. In a good way.

The Purge

A friend of mine recently admitted that she has 13,000 emails hanging out in her cyber-garage. Needless to say, I weep for her.

Not since the day she first logged in has she known that magical moment when there is nothing left in her inbox that requires her attention. That moment is called **Inbox Zero** and oh God, it feels good.

(Although here I should point out that much like the

phrase *Zero Fucks Given,* this term can be a bit misleading. Giving zero fucks would essentially mean you lived alone, naked and asleep in a sensory deprivation tank — which I suppose means you wouldn't get any email either, but that's not really a feasible outcome for anyone outside of a Philip K. Dick story. Getting all the way to literally zero messages in your inbox might be similarly unfeasible, but you can certainly get close.)

What you — and my friend, bless her heart — need to do is **purge, purge, purge.** And then flex your purging muscles on a daily or weekly basis to ensure you never have to devote more than a small amount of time to it ever again. The initial purge may take a whole day. If you have 13,000 emails, it could take a week. But if you're serious about getting your shit together in the long term, you have to strategize, focus, and commit in the short term. **Spend the time now to save it later.**

Here's what the Purge looks like:

Strategize: Get to zero (or close) messages by deleting, filing, or responding to everything currently in your inbox, in one fell swoop.

Focus: Reserve the necessary time in your calendar. Quick, before you get ten more emails! (If things are totally out of control, you can count your messages and tackle 10 per cent of them in one go, to estimate how long it will take you and how many Red Bulls you'll have to go the Full Monty.) You will no doubt have to *prioritize* the Purge over something less urgent, such as waxing your legs or... other things.

Pro tip: Purging early in the morning or late at night helps, since you're less likely to receive a ton of new messages while you're trying to get a handle on your current situation.

Commit: Start with **"Delete"** because it's so fucking easy. That's when you'll sit there with your down arrow key and trash icon fingers ready to stamp out expired airfare deals, Weight Watchers at Work sign-up sheets, and junk mail that you inexplicably didn't delete the moment it arrived. Were you planning to respond to that nice Nigerian man who asked you to wire him $300,000?

Sorting by sender is a gift—you can eradicate all the emails from Human Resources with a single stroke. Have you ever received a useful email from HR? Exactly.

Next, you'll need to **"File."** Your email program comes with a folder-adding feature. Trust me on this. So if there's a message that doesn't require action but you need access to it for posterity, you can create a folder and then file that shit away. My email folders have names like "Speaking invites," "Germany," and "Misc." (The miscellaneous folder functions like that drawer you shove all your sex toys into when your mother comes to visit. Very handy.)

Finally, it's **"Reply"** time. This is what you've been avoiding all along—telling people you "never got that email" or "haven't had time to look at it" because you either legit didn't see it among the 12,999 other messages or you prioritized that back-and-forth with your friend Tina about your UTI symptoms over, you know, actual work. Time to pour yourself a nice tall glass of cranberry juice and bang 'em out. Once separated from the herd, most will probably be pretty easy to spot and cull, but if a particular message is going to take a lot of thought/time to reply to, set it aside and schedule that as a single task on your must-do list for the week. (Just heed Polonius while you're at it.)

Butt in the seat, delete, delete, delete. Go the extra mile and file, file, file. Don't be that guy: Reply, reply, reply!

The day-to-day (or week-to-week)

Once you've successfully purged your way to Inbox Zero or thereabouts, catching up on email won't be a perennially looming disaster. It can just have **its own time slot, where you focus on it, and *only* it (X), for Y minutes or hours,** depending on your needs.

And if you have a Pavlovian reaction to the *ping* of notifications on your mobile phone or computer, you know you can turn those off, right? I used to do that when I wanted to edit at my desk without being interrupted, and I never missed an urgent message. All that shit was waiting for me after lunch when I was good and ready to deal with it. Of course, I worked in publishing. If you're a Google employee, they might court-martial you for that. It's a judgement call.

The key is time management, and knowing what your regular volume really looks like — not that insane backlog that you built up over the last six months. You can perform the 10 per cent purge I talked about, extrapolate, and then set aside whatever time you need to handle your email during your day or week. If you budget thirty minutes or two hours to do that (and nothing else), you'll be more organized, less frazzled, and will no longer have a reputation as That Guy Who Never Responds to My Emails.

Inbox Anxiety

Finally, I have **a special tip for all the Simons out there.**

Are you worried that if you step away from your email for too long, heads will roll, kingdoms will fall, the Chipmunks will never get booked for another gig, and it will be *all your fault*?

Then you have **Inbox Anxiety,** and I'm here to tell you that "pathological responsiveness," however tempting, is not the answer.

I know you think it is. So did I for, like, twenty years or however long email was around until I figured out I was trapped in the **Constant Cycle of Reply.** No end and no beginning, less gross than the Human Centipede, but equally tragic.*

For starters, pathologically responding to email the moment it comes in is textbook **reactive vs. proactive behaviour.** It's like treading water instead of swimming for shore — you're expending all that energy just to stay in one place. A bad place. An anxious place. You might as well wrap all those email chains around your ankles and sink right down to the bottom, because that's where you're headed anyway. If you engage in aggressive acts of delete-file-reply *all day long,* you'll never accomplish anything else, and you will drown. In email. Got it?

You'll probably also wind up responding too quickly to one message and realizing seconds (or an hour) later

---

* If you don't know what the Human Centipede is, I would not recommend looking it up. It's not a life you want to live.

that there was more to say, necessitating another email. Wait. **Don't be reactive.** Focus on it later, all at once, when you have time and energy to be thoughtful, strategic, and proactive. When you can respond with *just the facts, ma'am* and have time to *go all-inclusive.*

If you find yourself in the grip of Inbox Anxiety, try the "Stop, drop, and roll" exercise from page 90. Back slowly away from your device, take a deep breath, consult your must-do list, and remember: You'll get to your emails at 3:00 PM today, in between the dentist and drafting that press release.

The magic of scheduling ([cough] calendars [cough]) can free your mind from Inbox Anxiety.

That's some high-quality mental decluttering, right there.

Dialling it in

Want to see how many email fires you can put out without ever using your own hose? Pretend your twenty-first-century machine is a dial-up modem from 1987 — you could only

---

check those things twice a day because they took three hours just to connect!

If you limit the number of times you check/respond to email each day, you limit the constant background noise that's always interrupting and stealing your focus from other things. Instead, each "checking session" becomes its own concrete item on the must-do list.

And with enough lag time between log-ons, many questions will be answered by other people (be they work-related, or just where-are-we-meeting-for-dinner-related). Which then makes seventeen messages about the relative merits of Wahaca vs. Wagamama easy to delete the next time you "dial up." Plus margaritas, because Wahaca, *obviously*.

And although email is probably the most common, pervasive threat to getting your shit together, correspondence takes many forms. As I said earlier, after reading and taking this section to heart, you may find yourself thinking twice about sending that needless text or posting in Slack, lest you generate an avalanche of self-imposed distraction and Constant Cycle of Reply that leaves you unable to breathe, let alone get shit done.

It's tough being a human centipede.

Quittin' time: an experiment

That noise you just heard was me cracking my knuckles. (Don't worry, it sounds worse than it feels. But I appreciate your concern.)

I'm about to lay down a long-form example that will tie together everything we've learned so far about **goal-setting, motivation, must-do lists, time management, prioritizing, strategy, focus, and commitment.**

I'll start by giving you a hypothetical **What/Why** scenario and talk you through it step by step.

> **What's wrong with my life?** I spend too much time at work and I haven't seen Happy Hour in six months.
>
> **Why?** Whenever the word *time* is included in a statement about how shitty your life is, poor time management is probably the culprit. You *must* develop a better understanding of and relationship with time. (How'd that sundial installation go? Send pics!)
>
> **Goal:** Get your work done without having to stay late.

So, let's see...most days you find yourself at your desk (or a comparable post) two hours later than you intended, than you're expected to be there, or than you're being paid for. You're stuck in an overtime-shaped rut filled with complacency. Sounds like you need to get **motivated**.

Try **the Power of Negative Thinking** on for size:

- Do you hate working late?

- Does it make you angry?

- Do you spend your lunch break cooking up revenge fantasies involving Xerox machines, pornographic magazines, and your coworkers' family photos, which you could only implement if you stayed *even later*?

- Do you want to stop wasting time and energy on hatred, anger, and revenge fantasies, and instead put that time and energy into getting your work done so you can peace out before Happy Hour is but a distant memory?

I thought as much. Let's apply a little **GYST Theory** to this situation. Keys, phone, wallet: Report!

Goal: Get your work done without having to stay late.

Strategize: Turn your to-do list into a must-do list. By *planning* out your tasks and *prioritizing* them, you've broken your day up into small, manageable chunks instead of one giant blob of indistinguishable urgency. This minimizes the work you *need* to get done, and if you're trying to cram less into your day, you're bound to finish sooner.

(If getting out of work on time is actually a problem for you—and I didn't choose it as my hypothetical because it's such a fucking rare complaint—give the **Must-Do Method** a shot in the space below, or on the scrap paper of your choosing.

ALL THE SHIT I HAVE TO DO AT WORK IN THE FORESEEABLE FUTURE

_____
_____
_____
_____
_____
_____
_____
_____

ALL THE SHIT I HAVE TO DO AT WORK **IN ORDER OF URGENCY**

_____
_____
_____
_____
_____
_____
_____

ALL THE SHIT I **MUST** DO TODAY

_____
_____
_____
_____
_____

Focus: This is where *time management* comes in. You whittled your list down from ten items to five, but remember that *focusing* is about setting aside a realistic amount of time in which to get a task done AND using that time exclusively to complete that task. **SINGLE-TASKING!** In order to focus effectively, you have to know how *long it takes* to complete those single tasks. Of course there will be fluctuations in your workday, but if you've improved your time management chops, you'll be able to instinctively tailor your task-to-time ratio as events unfold.*

Commit: You've laid out the must-do items. You've set aside the time in which to do each of them. Now you have to bust out your metaphorical wallet and pay the piper. Sit down (or stand up, or hang suspended in mid-air — maybe you're an astronaut?) and DO THIS SHIT. This is where **the Power of Negative Thinking** will continue to serve you well. You already used it to help you formulate your goal — you were tired of

* This skill reverberates into every single area of your life: No longer will you miss the appetizers, the last bus, or the first fifteen minutes of a movie because you just didn't give yourself enough time to *get there.*

being chained to your desk (or spaceship) long after the workday had allegedly ended. You hated missing out on fun plans because you were always "just finishing up"…for three hours. You channelled those negative feelings into action. Keep it up!

If you need more *motivation* to commit to the plan, summon those feelings of fatigue and FOMO and combat them by completing one small, manageable goal at a time, crossing things off your must-do list, and leaving work not only on schedule, but with a new-found feeling of accomplishment and joyful anticipation of your first half-price martini in months.

There's a reason they don't call it Sad Hour.

The midday ambush

Whether it's a busted jar of pickles in aisle three or a surprise visit from the CEO, shit happens that you may have to deal with on the fly. That means you need to *prioritize* on the fly as well. If you've worked the must-do list, your shit should be together enough to survive a sneak attack. Theodores can emerge from under the bed. Alvins can remain in the building. And Simons can carry on without popping six Xanax. A hidden benefit: It's possible you didn't prioritize as much as

---

you could have for today already, and the TRUE same-day emergency will show you there was something that didn't belong on your must-do list after all.

The money shot

Along with time and energy, money is one of the three core resources at your disposal that can make or break your winning run at life. **And money is the only resource that keeps on giving.** Less money can be spent, more money can be made. And pre-existing money can sit in a high-interest account and *make itself* while you sleep and/ or zone out to Food Network.

I know so many people — some who make less money than I do, and some who make a lot more — who complain about their finances. Who lament not being able to pay for or save for this or that. They think of money as a lion that can't be tamed. Or worse, as a cute, fuzzy little mogwai in the streets and a gremlin in the sheets.

In reality, money is just a piece of paper and you're a real live human being with free will and probably at least two pairs of sneakers. If you're someone who says **"I can't make it to payday without dipping into my savings"** or **"I'm always spending a little bit more than I should,"** then you're allowing money to build a prison around you and make you its bitch.

What I'm saying is, **Don't be money's bitch.**

You need to manage your money, not the other way around. Entire books have been written on this subject* by economists and wealth managers and self-made millionaires and guys named Jim. But if money management were all you needed help with, you probably would have gone to that shelf in the bookstore. Instead, you came to me. Why? Because I promised to teach you how to get your shit together in a broad, sweeping fashion, one that includes but is not limited to your financial life.

And so I shall.

The secret is: **They're all the same secrets.**

We just used a combination of strategy, focus, and commitment to shorten your workday. Now we'll do the

---

* At Amazon, there are currently 73,257 results for books on "money management."

same to **pad your bank account and enable lifestyle goals you once thought were out of reach — through a mix of less spending and more saving.**

Hey, Big Spender

Whether your goal is tall (hot pair of shoes to wear to your ten-year high school reunion), grande (diamond bracelet to flash at twenty-year high school reunion), or venti (tummy tuck in advance of thirty-year high school reunion), your strategy could be as easy as forgoing your $5

> **Lifestyle goals you may wish to achieve**
>
> Getting out of debt
> Fixing up your porch
> Owning a spiffy plaid suit
> Winning an eBay auction
> Making it rain at the Spearmint Rhino

Starbucks run for X days until you have the cash to hit Y goal.

- 30 days of focus and commitment = $150 in Vanilla Bean Crème Frappuccinos, or one pair of hot shoes

- 300 days for $1,500 worth of diamonds

- 1,200 days ($6,000) for a mid-price mid-section reduction

The same strategy can be applied to bigger things, like paying for your kid's orthodontics or university (or *your* orthodontics or university). Maybe even a down payment on a MINI Cooper. Those things are adorable.

But first, let's deal in a more universal hypothetical.

What's wrong with my life? I've noticed I'm a little bit in the red each month, and I don't like it.

Indeed. The feeling of watching your bank account get to, then dip below, zero is similar to the feeling of watching a teenager in a horror movie go back into the house where the murderer is *clearly* lying in wait.

Why? Um, I'm spending a little too much?

Yes! You're getting good at this. We'll call it $100. And I understand that $100 over the course of the month is not necessarily "a little too much" to some readers, but it's a round number and I am but a humble English major. Whatever your monthly deficit, I'm here to help you apply your new-found skills across a whole range of shit, relative to your own life and your own concept of winning. (Note: This hypothetical also supposes that the person in question can't figure out where that $100 is going, or he/she would have already stopped fucking spending it.)

> **Goal:** Spend $100 less each month. Don't go into the house. Don't tempt the murderer. Simple.

For that, you need to...

> **Strategize:** How about spending $25 less each week for four weeks? Each $25 increment is a smaller, more manageable chunk than the $100 total. Take it one chunk at a time.

That's called...

> **Focus:** This week, when you're confronted with a potential expenditure, think about how much it

costs, in increments of $25. Ask yourself, *Do I really need it?* If the answer is no, don't take out your wallet or swipe your credit card or sign your name on that dotted line.

Don't spend the money. This is known as…

Commitment: If you're reading *Maxim* and are tempted by the latest in bacon-scented moustache wax, but you don't need another jar of goo on your bathroom sink, don't buy it. That's $25 saved by resisting bacon's formidable charms. Going out to dinner? Mmmm…tasty. But stick to a main course and a drink — skip the appetizer and dessert (or vice versa). Hey, there's another $25 you didn't spend. You're now halfway to your goal. You may also be halfway to a weight loss goal. WHO KNOWS?!?

When I lay it out, this all seems so obvious, doesn't it? Yet a lot of people (a) never set a goal, and (b) if they do, get too overwhelmed by the size of it, so that (c) they can't focus on (d) committing.

No pennies left to pinch

On a serious note, I don't want to downplay the privilege inherent in the financial advice I'm giving. My assumption is that most people reading this book deemed it worthy of some disposable income — and that they therefore *have* some extra income to dispose of. But maybe you aren't sifting through impulse buys at the checkout line in TK Maxx so much as you're weighing the phone bill with one hand and a box of nappies with the other. Perhaps this book was a gift, or a library loan, or you spent what little disposable income you do have on it because you hoped it would help you make some big changes. If that's the case, first of all, thank you for reading. Second, I hope my advice comes across in the spirit in which it's intended, rather than making you feel minimized or excluded. And third, I hope you enjoyed the irritable bowel syndrome joke on page 64. I was proud of that one.

If you've never really focused on your weekly expenses, then you may not have realized that moustache wax or tiramisu were the $25 — times four — that became your monthly shortfall. (Even better, multiplied by fifty-two weeks, that's a cool $1,300 you just found in the metaphorical couch cushions for the year.)

Now let's make it even easier.

Let's say this $100-a-month debt is haunting you like that creepy fucker from the perplexingly well-reviewed movie *It Follows,* but even $25 a week doesn't feel like a small enough, manageable enough goal to keep it at bay. So you break your chunks down further, into a *daily* amount.

That works out to $3.57 you need to NOT spend each day, for a month, to account for your $100 shortfall.

Now I'm going to ask you to focus for a hot second on where you spend your money every day. Maybe it would help to…I don't know…make a list? If you do (and again, assuming you have disposable income but just can't get a handle on where it runs off to each month), it's highly likely that you'll find $3.57 on that list that can be eliminated easily and **with zero, or minimal, negative impact on your quality of life.**

But for the umpteenth time, chipmunks, I'm not here to police your spending habits or tell you what the correct (or

---

Five things on which you don't need to spend $3.57 (or more)

A cup of coffee
Two Lottery tickets
A 3-pack of gum
A collapsible shot glass key chain
Any three-and-a-half items from the dollar store

---

incorrect) priorities are for your life. I'm just trying to show you that if you **think about your spending habits as smaller parts of the whole—pennies on the dollar, you might say**—you can get your individual, unique, personal financial shit together too.

Oh, and when you're ready to attack your finances, it may be worth the $3.57 to invest in another notebook, to monitor your daily expenses. (The Procrastination Journal is a sacred space.) By recording everything you spend, you're forced to confront your decisions, and it will be easier to start making better ones *before* you come home from the clothes swap with a pair of shoes that don't fit and a bobbly cardigan.

We bought a zoo

Cool, so we've talked about NOT spending. Now let's talk about ACTIVELY saving. The single biggest financial mistake people make is thinking about putting away some savings and then saying "I'll start tomorrow."

They do that because **the end goal seems too enormous to contemplate today.**

Well, I've shown you what kind of difference $3.57 can make today, or $25 can make this week, or $100 can make this month. If you put aside all of that extra cash, you could take those few bucks a week and, **over the course of many, many weeks,** put them toward something that brings you a fuck-ton of joy.

A trip to Disney World. A new car. A down payment on a zoo. Or just a house, which is probably more practical.

Still on the fence? It might help to think of your savings plan like **a piggy bank with a slot only big enough for a quarter.** Nobody's asking you to shove a brick of Jane Austens in there all at once. No, the easiest and most effective way to reach your big, long-term lifestyle goal is in small, manageable chunks. And when you do it this way, it's just not that hard. Switching careers is hard. Overcoming addiction is hard. Caring for elderly parents is hard. Saving a few thousand bucks is not terribly hard—all it takes is…wait for it…**strategy, focus,** and **commitment.**

And **time.** Which means, yes, this kind of goal-setting also calls for **patience.**

The Alvins of the world don't have that kind of

attention span, which is why I implore them to break such a goal up into small, manageable chunks so they *can* focus on it a little bit every day rather than running for the hills at the first mention of a "three-year plan."

I've told you about my experience of saving money in order to be able to quit my job and begin working as a freelancer, as well as to build a house in the Caribbean. Woo-hoo! No more drab conference rooms, no more blistering high heels, and unlimited access to ice-cold Presidente Light. I better take some ibuprofen if I'm going to keep patting myself on the back so hard, right?

But the outcome, however fabulous, is not what I want to emphasize here. What I want to convey to you about this whole deal was: IT TOOK A LONG TIME. Hell, it took a long time just to *set* those goals. They were pretty big. Life-changing, you might say. Once I did set them, it's not like I could act on them same-day. (Well, not responsibly, anyway.)

That's where my strategy came in, and as mentioned, it wound up requiring **a full year of saving** to get where I needed to be. Three hundred and sixty-five days of taking a small amount of money and putting it into a savings account.

If you're an Alvin, your eyes may be glazing over right

about now, but stay with me for a sec, because this is all about **perspective.**

Human beings **pay money and then wait for shit to happen all the time,** right? We get charged up front for season tickets and then have to recoup our investment over the course of many months (especially long months if you're a Sunderland FC fan). We pony up the monthly Hulu fee and then wait forever for ten new episodes of the lone TV show that we got the membership to watch. Millions of people have been giving George R. R. Martin their hard-earned cash and untold hours of their attention for years and they may *never* find out what happens to the bastard spawn of Westeros if he doesn't write those last two books.

Surely a down payment on a zoo/home of your own (or a fabulous getaway, or a set of amazing rims) is worth exercising some patience, no? The only difference is **the amount of money and time standing between you and your goal,** which is what makes this aspect of getting your shit together relatively easy.

Have more money to sock away per day = Take less time to reach the goal

Have less money to sock away per day = Take more time to reach the goal

Either way—and whether you need to save $100 or $100,000 to pay a mechanic or buy a yacht (half a yacht?)—the goal eventually gets reached.

You got this.

A spoonful of willpower helps the medicine go down

Before we move on to part III and the tough shit, there's one more component of getting your shit together whose significance cannot be ignored: **willpower.**

I'm afraid this one's on you.

I can give you the motivational tricks and tips on time management. I can simplify the steps and I can put a charmingly obscene twist on the self-help genre to keep your spirits up. But I can't inhabit your brain and body and *make* you follow my advice. If I could do that, I would have a reality show and a lip kit line by now.

Only you can get your shit together, set your goals, and go forth and win at life — your life, whatever that involves. To stay committed to those goals, you're gonna need some willpower.

But it's only a little bit of willpower at a time! Enough to focus and complete those small, manageable parts of your plan. And you can summon willpower in different ways, depending on what works for you.

THE ART OF ~~WAR~~ WILLPOWER

IF YOU'RE MOTIVATED BY		USE THIS STRATEGY
Money	→	The Scrooge McDuck *Envision yourself rolling around in piles of all that loot you're saving/not spending.*
Vanity	→	The Photo Finish *Taping a picture of your thinner self to the fridge isn't the worst way to shut down the Wizard of Impulse Control.*

IF YOU'RE MOTIVATED BY		USE THIS STRATEGY
Adulation	→	The Ego Boost *Life-winners are often admired by their peers. If that appeals to you, use it as fuel.*
Getting pissed off	→	The Power of Negative Thinking *Good for lighting a fire and keeping it hot.*
Accountability	→	The "Who Raised You?" *Gives you a swift kick in the pants, just like Mum used to.**

Each of these strategies is useful at different times under different circumstances, but that last one really helps when you find yourself up shit creek without a paddle.

As it turns out, **accountability can be highly motivating.**

---

* I'm using *Mum* as a generic term for the person who raised you. If you were reared by a single dad, an older sibling, a grandparent, or a sentient raccoon, by all means, substitute accordingly.

Now, some people might correlate accountability with "shame" or "caring what other people think," but I contend that there are a few (if not fifty) shades of grey in between. **I don't give a fuck about what other people think of my life choices**—in the sense that it doesn't bother me if someone disapproves of my actions, as long as I know I'm acting in my own best interests.

I don't need to feel ashamed of that, and neither do you.

But what if I don't *realize* that my actions are hurting me? What if I were stumbling blindly through life—stuck in a bad job, bad relationship, or really unflattering haircut—and I didn't know it? What if somebody pointed it out to me and gave me the tough love, complete with paddle, to help me turn things around?

An emotional spanking

Apart from sexual submissives, nobody likes being told what to do. But periodically stepping out of your mental bubble to see yourself through another person's eyes can be a low-impact gut check. *Who raised you?* is my second-favourite thing to think/mutter when I encounter someone making poor life choices. And while I intend it sarcastically—as though given

---

their lack of self-control/hygiene/manners they might have been brought up by a pair of outlaw raccoons — it's actually a good question to ask if you haven't had much luck being accountable to *yourself* lately.

If you have a hard time mustering or sustaining willpower — especially for the tough shit — you may be subconsciously looking for someone else to beat it into you. Practising "Who Raised You?" helps you recognize the behaviours that would cause your mother (or your dominatrix) to say, "For fuck's sake, get your shit together."

Who raised you? works like this:

If you wonder: *Why can't I get a girl to spend the night, let alone develop a meaningful relationship with me?*

Ask yourself: *Would my mum approve of the nest of dirty boxer shorts I've built on my bed in lieu of doing laundry? If not, why would* any *woman?*

If you wonder: *Why is everyone getting promoted except me?*

Ask yourself: *What would my mum say if she knew I spent half the day on* Bachelorette *message boards instead of doing my job?*

If you wonder: *Why can't I afford nice things?*

Ask yourself: *Would my mum be proud to know that every month my paycheck gets spent almost exclusively on weed and eyedrops?*

Yes, an emotional spanking might be just the ticket. Or a real one, if that works. You do you, Theo. (I'm still not judging.)

TOUGH SHIT:
Getting older, getting ahead, getting healthy, and getting better at life in general

This isn't so bad, is it? We're making excellent progress. By now, you're an old pro at must-do lists, your inbox is on fleek, and you might even have an extra $100 burning a hole in your bank account. You've learned the value of prioritizing, the workday is looking more manageable, and you finally know how long it really takes you to shower and shave.

Congratulations! **You're well on your way to winning at life** (and without being an insufferable prick, I might add).

If you're a Theodore, "I don't know where to start" should no longer be in your vocabulary, nor should "There's too much on my list." Now we're moving into what I think of as Alvin territory — stuff that requires a longer attention span or protracted commitment. Though it must be said, all chipmunks can and will benefit from part III, which (as is my wont) is further broken down into three smaller, more manageable categories:

- **Responsibilities & Relationships:** Being an adult AND acting like one.

- **Work & Finances:** Looking to get promoted? Look no further! Also: Delegating, enjoying your time off, and saving for retirement.

- **Health, Home & Lifestyle:** Staying hale and hearty so you can *make it* to retirement; keeping your house clean after you clean it; the ways in which *Changing Rooms* is lying to you and the benefits of hiring a pro; and carving out time for hobbies and creative pursuits.

Oh, I'm sorry, Alvin, did you think I was fucking around?

SURPRISE!

I'm not.

Responsibilities & Relationships

In this section, we'll explore "adulting" — a term I did not coin but wish I had. Getting your shit together isn't all email and piggy banks; you also need to go to the doctor and renew your passport and learn to dispatch annoying chores with skill and vigour. Stop paying late fees and start writing thank-you notes. And in between all of that stuff, you have to find time to spend on your friends, family, and/or people you're having sex with. (But only if you really want to. Per usual, I'm not telling you what to do here — only how you might go about it, if you deem it important to your overall happiness.) Perhaps you're more interested in getting *out of* a relationship — like, for good, not just for this weekend. In that case, keep reading, but I wouldn't leave this book lying out on the coffee table open to page 160. Rookie mistake.

For adults only

When I was ten, I traded V. C. Andrews books back and forth with my older cousin. At the time, I didn't understand all the "adult stuff" that was in them, but I did learn valuable lessons, such as "never underestimate what people will do for an inheritance" and "if the only thing you're eating all day is powdered donuts, you're probably going to get sick."

In the same way, I hope there are some kids out there getting very excited about this next section. It's not X-rated (sorry), but it *is* informative, and reading it now will make your lives vastly easier upon entry into the world of parking meters and prostate exams.

Life's a pitch

Part of winning at life is dealing with shit that suddenly demands urgent attention. A three-year-old who steps on a rusty nail at the playground typically has a teacher, parent, or babysitter there to calm them down, dust them off, apply the antibacterial ointment, and make a follow-up appointment for a tetanus shot. When you're an adult and these things happen, you have to deal with it your own damn self. (Note to own damn self: Add Savlon to the grocery list.)

But a rusty nail, unpleasant though it may be when introduced to your foot, doesn't have to put the whole Game of Life in jeopardy.

I know, it sucks to feel like you finally mastered your daily routine — fastball up in the strike zone — **and then life throws you a curve.** Luckily, everything you've learned so far about better time management, prioritizing, and impulse control has prepared you for this shit.

You're already more efficient, right? You're not running late all the time. Your days are better structured and therefore more relaxed. In fact, you're hitting fastballs out of the park in your sleep — which means you have more time, energy, and money to spare for the other pitches life hurls your way, be they curves, sliders, or a really filthy changeup.

Such pitches may include:

The Unusual Expense

We've talked about the daily dollar, about understanding how much you spend (and on what), in order to rein in your expenses and beef up your savings. But what about the occasional costs, like tux rentals or parking tickets? These don't appear in the daily or even monthly calculations because they are so infrequent, but you can't let their infrequency render them somehow less urgent when they do occur. And just because you haven't trained yourself to settle a parking ticket every day doesn't mean you should be any less swift and decisive when it appears twice a year on your must-do list. People who have their shit together don't pay late fees.

The Doctor's Appointment

Maybe you're a rare specimen of genetic perfection and see no need to keep up with annual physicals and the ritual sadism of dentistry, which is fine. If it ain't broke, don't fix it. But someday, you're going to be told by a medical professional that you need to "get that checked out" (or worse: "taken care of"), and that appointment is going to hang over your head like a guillotine blade until you just fucking MAKE IT. Yes, it's annoying. Yes, it may be an awkward call to place if you happen to be in an open-plan office surrounded by coworkers. And yes, the prospect of getting your bum palpated by a middle-aged version of your cousin Steve is unappetizing (at best). But for the sake of your health — not to mention your must-do list — you have to duck outside, make the call, budget the time, and show up. People who have their shit together don't suffer needlessly.

The Expired Passport

Do not pass "go." Do not get to the airport check-in before you realize your passport is out of date. Get your shit together.

The Thank-You Note

Hi. I'm an adult, you're an adult, let's act like adults. If someone does something nice for you, say thank you. If they do something extra nice for you, say thank you in writing. The good karma you get from the universe by sending a card is worth the three minutes out of your day it takes to write one and stick it in the mail. But most especially, if you're on the receiving end of a pile of presents — wedding, baby shower, graduation, whatever — get your shit together and write the thank-you notes before you even start using your gifts. I wrote all my wedding thank-you notes in the airport waiting to board the plane for my honeymoon, which meant every subsequent margarita came with a guilt-free rim.

The Annoying Chore

For me this typically involves going to the post office, which is a rare errand in a world ruled by email and Jeff Bezos. I hate the post office. Nothing good has ever happened to me in a post office, and in fact, I have cried there on several occasions. But you can't let your abject hatred of Royal Mail stop you from having your shit together. Because if you avoid annoying chores long enough, you'll wind up spending $32 to overnight Priority Mail your grandfather's two-dollar birthday card, and that's just stupid. That is the antithesis of having your shit together. You still had to go to the post office *and* your dilly-dallying cost you thirty bucks. *Jesus, Sarah, get your shit together.*

Whether the preceding has been an **Intro to Adulting** or simply a refresher course, I hope you found it useful. Acting like an adult is part and parcel of having your shit together, and it's the only way you're ever going to get out of your parents' house, *stay* out, and then become one of those people who tells kids how hard everything was "back in my day." Did you know that my father picked blueberries for a nickel a bushel? Well, he did. And my first job was working for a comedy website where we had a dartboard and a singing plastic fish mounted on the wall, BUT we had no drinks dispenser, so there was still room for me to move up in the world.

As there is for you.

Righting the relation-ship

Another part of being an adult is building relationships. When you're a kid, you just sort of hang out with your parents' friends' kids, or the neighbours, or anyone who has a pool in their garden. As you get older and your peer group diversifies, you start to make more concrete decisions about who you want to spend your time with, and why. By the time adulthood fully sets in, you're embroiled in a host of complex relationships — many by choice, others...not so much.

Whether with a friend, family member, or romantic liaison, relationships fall into three categories:

Maintain

Improve

Dissolve

Maintaining or improving requires some effort. For example, if you're meeting up with a buddy, leave your phone in your pocket. Live-tweeting your drinks date is distracting to both of you. If you're on the phone with your grandmother, she shouldn't have to hear Radio 1 playing in the background. Listen to her, not Nick Grimshaw.

Single-tasking shows you care.

Of course, you can't **focus** on or **commit** to anybody if you're never available, which is why you have to **prioritize** seeing and talking to these folks in the first place.

Missed connections

We've discussed being "too busy" to "do everything," and this is an excuse that is constantly levelled when we can't manage to get together with friends as often as we might like.

It's tough, for example, when you're just out of university and flung halfway across the country (or the globe) from people you used to fall asleep on at parties. You're starting a new life and suddenly have to worry about things like "jobs" and "rent" and you have neither the free time nor the credit card limit to be jaunting off to Edinburgh, to visit your old roommate who inexplicably decided to do a Master's in Scotland. You have Facebook, so you can overtly or covertly spy on each other (plus on the guy who nearly came between you in second year), and you still text a lot, but it's not the *same*.

Alas, it doesn't get any easier as you progress through your twenties, making new friends in a new city and at a new job, trying to fit them in too. Plus, if you have a significant other, his or her friends start encroaching on your nights and weekends like groupies on the Jonas brothers (mostly Nick, let's be real). You might even like a lot of those people, but they don't necessarily mix with your other friends, and then you and your paramour have to make difficult decisions about whose party to *start* with on Saturday night and where you want to end up — aka decide whose friends throw better parties. Relationships are hard.

After ten years of this, maybe in multiple cities and after multiple significant others, you've collected a few dozen more friends (and at least 200 Facebook friends), and now they're all getting married on the same weekend. Fuuuuuck.

Fast-forward *another* ten years, and most of your friends have kids — maybe you do too — and somehow even getting together for dinner with people who live in the same town as you involves a strategy worthy of the Lord of Catan. Slowly but surely, you fall out of touch. What was your university roommate's last name again? Miller?

Or maybe the "falling out of touch" happens once you take the last exit to Empty Nestville and realize it was all your kids' football games and bar mitzvahs and graduations and weddings that were *keeping* you in touch with friends. Now you're driving through unfamiliar territory with only a beat-up issue of *Saga* magazine as your guide.

It's perfectly natural for some friendships to fall by the wayside, at any stage of life. **The challenge is maintaining (or improving) the ones that are really important to you.** The ones that are worth the distance, the scheduling difficulties, the new kind of parties that start at noon and by 3:00 PM your friend's *kid* falls asleep on *you*.

The first step is to **be honest with yourself about whether this friendship IS worth it.** If not, I refer you to a different book entirely.* But if you decide it is, then you

---

* This one: www.lifechangingmagicofnotgaf.com.

can set a goal to maintain or improve it, and lay out a strategy for doing so.

For example, when I'm writing to a strict deadline, my priorities shift from "hang out with friends" to "get work done." I become a bit of a hermit, which is fine in shortish bursts, but I don't want to let it get out of hand, because that's how valued friends disappear from your life. It's like celebrity couples who are always breaking up because the distance between their fancy film sets is too much for true love (and apparently, private planes) to overcome.

So, my **strategy** has been to make a running list — shocker, I know — of all the fine peeps I've been putting off since I started writing *Get Your Shit Together*. It's the "People to See" entry in my AnyList app, under "Things We Should Probably Get Rid Of" and above "New Travel Toiletries."

I did this not because I wouldn't remember my friends' names otherwise, but as a visual reminder that not only do I *want* to see them, I *need* to make the time for it (i.e., **focus**) as soon as I'm out of Deadline Mode. And then I **commit** to an interim "Hey, just wanted you to know I'm thinking about you and really looking forward to cocktails when I come up for air" email.

Who doesn't like to get a nice email saying they're being thought of? A one-line note can really reset the clock on "Maybe this person doesn't value my friendship."

One line. It takes very little focus and commitment to type a one-line email.

So is your friendship worth it, or not?

"Hi" maintenance is low-maintenance

With family, things might be a little more complicated. Just a touch. A hint. A smidge.

Perhaps you have a sibling or parent whom you don't feel (or want to feel) very close to, but for whatever reason, you do give a fuck about maintaining the relationship. Can't live with 'em, can't live without 'em — I totally get it. Well, presumably you perform maintenance on other shit all the time, right? Like brushing your teeth, taking allergy medication, or shaving your legs. These tasks don't take long, and they contribute to your overall goals of remaining minty fresh, sneeze-free, and smooth like Santana.

In such cases, you could think of your relationship with your family member like you think of your relationship with your leg hair. You don't want things to get all prickly, so every few days you take a razor to it for ten minutes (a light email or quick call), or once a month you visit a stern Polish lady who spends half an hour ripping it out from the follicles (Skype).

Wish you were here!

Postcards are the perfect vehicle for at-a-distance relationship maintenance. You're on vacation—which means you're in the best possible place to deal with your family, i.e., very far away from them, generally relaxed and happy, and without much other shit to do—and dashing off a short note limited to about two square inches of text is an easy, easy way to show you're thinking of them. Cheap, too. Get your shit together and get thee to the gift shop, I say.

Then there are family members you simply don't *know* very well, like faraway cousins or little kids. You may not give a fuck about attending a wedding in Cumbria (though you hear it's beautiful) or sitting through a middle school production of *Guys and Dolls,* but you still feel it's important to show, somehow, that you care.

Time to strategize, focus, and commit.

Want to honour your cousin Deborah's nuptials? Decide on your budget, take ten minutes to peruse her online registry, and let your Amex do the talking. If Debbie doesn't have a registry (or you don't have a computer), nothing says "Congrats" like a nice Curry's gift card.

Want to make your nephew's day? Sending a "Break a leg" text (or even a Snapchat, if you have any idea what that is) would show you were thinking of him — and both of those take a lot less time and energy than keeping a straight face while watching a horde of tone-deaf twelve-year-olds perform "Sit Down, You're Rockin' the Boat."

The Relationship Relay

One thing I did not address in *The Life-Changing Magic of Not Giving a Fuck* was romantic relationships, and this omission becomes more glaring every time I get a Facebook message from a reader asking me how to stop giving a fuck about the stupid things her husband does.* Maybe

---

* Actual text of a recent message: "How do I stop giving a fuck about the stupid things my husband does?!"

I need to write *The Life-Changing Magic of Not Giving a Fuck for Newlyweds and/or Couples Living in Sin,* but for now you're just going to have to get your shit together and make it work — **if, that is, you want to maintain or improve your romantic union.**

Did you know that the Chipmunks have girlfriends? The Chipettes. Frustratingly heteronormative, perhaps, but useful for the purposes of this extended metaphor.

As do any romantic partners, Alvin and Brittany, Simon and Jeanette, and Theodore and Eleanor have their ups and downs. It's all pretty tame — these are cartoon chipmunks, after all — but sometimes they're super-sweet, and other times they're plotting to beat each other's asses in a hot-air balloon race around the world.

Tapping into your inner competitor is useful for obvious things like winning hot-air balloon races, but it can improve your love life, too. It's true, and I speak from experience. (This is not to say that I would ever compete in an actual sport with my husband; if we got recruited for, say, doubles tennis, we'd have to repair our marriage *plus* my sprained ankle long after I caused us to lose by virtue of being almost unfathomably uncoordinated.)

But I have found a different way to make competition—within a relationship—fun and rewarding. It's all about **being the best partner you can be, back and forth, in perpetuity.** Like a relationship relay. Who can be nicer, more helpful, or more loving on any given day? Who can come up with the perfect gift or the perfectly timed surprise? In a competition like this, everybody wins! And not that kind of "everybody wins" like in kindergarten when teachers hand out gold stars for not pooping in the sandbox two days running.

Some days are better than others. I'm not always my best self, and neither is he, but the very fact that we have this ongoing rivalry that involves doing nice things for each other puts us way ahead of the game when times are tough. **It's hard to stay mad at someone who spontaneously rubs your feet twice a week.**

(By the way, the general concept works wonders even if you're the only one playing. Fewer foot rubs for you, though.)

Whether you're in the puppy love stage or the golden years, injecting some healthy competition into your relationship is, well, healthy. And it **bleeds into other aspects of your life.** Suddenly taking out the rubbish is a favour you're doing for your girlfriend, as opposed to an annoying chore. Isn't that a nicer way to look at it? And the note she slipped inside your lunch put a smile on your face during the shittiest of workdays. (Why yes, your boss *should* suck a hard-boiled egg not unlike the ones used to make this sandwich.)

If your goal is happiness and harmony, just keep your keys, phone, and wallet in sight at all times.

Strategize: Devise ways to make your significant other feel good. Some of these could be extravagant — if/when you're feeling flush — but most can and should be as simple as keeping an emergency tub of Ben & Jerry's Bourbon Brown Butter in the freezer at all times. Or just a bottle of bourbon. Make a list and refer to it for inspiration as needed.

Focus: A small kindness worked in every day is better than one big "Ah, shit, I've been ignoring you" gift. (But those have their place too. See above: *Some of these could be extravagant.*)

Commitment: Say the words, do the deeds, and when in doubt, splurge on hugs.

Relationships need time and energy in order to thrive—this is not a package of sea monkeys you're raising in an old mayonnaise jar. But if you put more of that time and energy into doing nice things for each other, you waste less on petty arguments and competitive sulking. They don't give out trophies for that shit.

Strategize, focus, [de]commit

As I have demonstrated time and again, not giving a fuck goes a long way toward eliminating any number of people from your life. It's definitely possible to passively dissolve a relationship by slowly starving it of interaction—no name-calling or disinheriting necessary.

Actively dissolving a relationship is another matter, though you still needn't resort to name-calling. What you can resort to—or, rather, what you should embrace with the zeal of a thousand *Bachelor* contestants let loose in Tiffany's—is **getting your shit together to extricate yourself from a toxic or simply unwanted bond.**

There are a million-and-seven reasons a relationship—whether romantic, platonic, or familial—can go south.

Distance, betrayal, or simply chronic incompatibility. Wanting things the other person can't or won't give. One of you is a Trump supporter and the other one isn't a fan of bigoted narcissists who do teeny-weeny fist bumps over the prospect of nuclear war. These things happen.

If they happen to YOU, then I'm sorry to hear that. But it's going to be okay.

If the relationship is with someone with whom you thought you were going to spend your life (or at least every Christmas), the goal to dissolve it might be tough to set. Meeting it might be tough too, but **there are ways to *mitigate* the level of toughness, and make things easier on yourself.** Like, it's definitely going to hurt when you get that IUD put in, but swallowing four ibuprofen beforehand and arranging to take the rest of the day off from work will help. You just gotta think ahead or, hmmmm...what's that word...

Strategize!

What does getting out of this relationship look like? After the first difficult conversation, how many logistics will there be between you and never dealing with this person again—or in arranging the coparenting of your children or cats? Are you going to have to pack your things and go, or do you just never have to *go* anywhere at all, i.e., to their house for the holidays?

I don't mean to treat the dissolution of a lifelong or even five-year-long relationship as some kind of petty nuisance. That's not fair to you, or your Republican uncle. But summoning my best Scarlett O'Hara, I do declare that **however complex the situation is, it can always be broken down into smaller, more manageable chunks.**

Next, set yourself a time frame and focus on each chunk as it comes. Then, commit.

Or decommit, as the case may be.

Nobody puts Baby in the culturally acceptable corner

Oh, and here's a novel idea: How about not committing at all (to a romantic relationship)? That's okay too! **You can be hot shit all by yourself,** no matter what big old box of "should" your family, friends, or society in general may be trying to stuff you into. Being single is fine. Dating around is fine. YOU CAN EVEN ALTERNATE. And while I'm at it, here's a list of other stuff you don't have to do just because other people think you *should*:

Be heterosexual

Be gender-conforming

Get married

Register for monogrammed towels

Have 2.5 children

Own a house

Get rid of your Hotmail address

You should, however, take my advice. All of it. No exceptions.

Work & Finances

As you know, a big part of getting my shit together the last few years was quitting my job to work for myself. But YOU might be as happy as the proverbial clam in your current gig — so happy, in fact, that you just want to get a raise or get promoted, not give it all up for a bag of coconuts and a pet spider. That's awesome and I support you. (More coconuts for me.) This section is about not merely maintaining, but *improving* your work life — from elevating your spot in the pecking order to learning how to enjoy a hard-earned vacation. First stop on that train: Delegation Station! I'll also show you how the money you're working so hard for now can serve you even better in the long run, because compound interest makes you rich. Or at least makes it so you don't have to keep drawing a paycheck well into your eighties, which is a goal most people can get all aboard with.

Skills include

No matter what your job looks like — a traditional career track or something fabulously unusual — there are those you will have to impress on your way to the top. And what's more impressive than having your shit together? Forget "Basic facility with Photoshop and conversational French." People should actually list "I have my shit together" on their CVs. I'd hire those people.

In *Part II: Theodore Does Details* we covered a lot of self-management techniques with regard to your working life (time, to-do lists, revenge fantasies). And of course showing up bright and early and hitting deadlines will come in handy no matter what. But if you're looking to nab a raise or a promotion, to win the big client, or to get a Nobel Prize or whatever, you've come to the right place. I have relevant experience in some, if not all, of these arenas.*

---

* Someday, Nobel Committee. Someday.

Be a con(fidence) man

Looking confident — even if inside, you're scared shitless — is a great way to gain the trust and respect of your boss or clients and get ahead. Later in the book we'll talk more about how to combat anxiety and other self-defeating mental states that might be shaking your confidence, but for now we're just going to work with *appearances*.

Inside, you may be Verbal Kint, but outside, **you've got to be Keyser Söze.**

I know, this doesn't come naturally to the Theodores among you. It's hard to be (or look) confident when you feel like the world is falling down around you at all times. Hopefully the advice I've doled out thus far has helped alleviate that feeling and freed you up to try calm, cool, and collected on for size. I hear it's all the rage this season.

Alvins are actually pretty good at the confidence game already. They have a lot of energy to divert to *looking* self-possessed while they get their shit together to match the carpet to the drapes. If you're an Alvin, you may be closer than you think to those Deputy Director business cards you've had your eye on.

Simons can be truly confident (on the cusp of Alvin) or

not (first house in Theodore); either way they are usually high-functioning enough to gain the trust — but sometimes also the abuse — of clients and higher-ups. If you're a member of the Brotherhood of the Blue Turtleneck, getting ahead in your career may be more about strategizing your own time and energy to avoid getting sidetracked by *quantity* of tasks in favour of *quality* of work.

In any case, if need be, you can start **projecting confidence** by mastering a few key phrases such as:

No problem.

Got you covered.

I'm on it!

And graduate to ones like:

Making Shit Happen is my middle name.

You can also engage in some harmless **confidence cosplay.** Observe your coworkers. Who looks like they've got their shit together? What makes you think that about them? Perhaps their cheerful demeanour, their steady hands, or the fact that their shirt doesn't have yesterday's $.99 burrito bowl all over it. Is there any reason you can't look like that too? All I'm saying is, an inordinate number of people spend time and money dressing up like Walter White and Sexy Jesse every Halloween; I have to believe this kind of effort could be expended to more beneficial results.

Ask and ye shall receive

A lot of gurus and life coaches and people with opinions will tell you that you have to "ask for what you want." That's fine, but I think you should also **ask what you have to do to get what you want.** I mean *literally ask* your boss or clients, "What do I have to do to get you to give me what I want?"

Take the mystery out of this shit!

I have watched so many people languish in their careers, waiting for someone above them to give a hint as to what it takes to unlock that corner office. And I have watched so many managers and CEOs pay absolutely no attention to the needs or desires of their underlings until they absolutely have to — usually when said underling gives notice.

Raises and promotions can be approached like any

other goal, except that — BONUS — by asking your boss or clients to **provide you with a clear strategy** (e.g., "Sign fifty new accounts in one year" or "Take someone under your wing and show me that you can be a good manager"), *you* can proceed straight to **focus** and **commitment**.

BOOM: You just eliminated the middle man. That's Deputy Director material!

Not to mention, this gambit has the added benefit of highlighting when there may not *be* any room for promotion or extra pay. If you make this kind of ask and your boss huffs and puffs or dodges and weaves, well, that tells you something. Sometimes people languish not because they're not *capable* of advancement — but because there *is* no way forward and they just don't know it. Why? They haven't asked.

If your boss tells you there's nothing you can do, or simply tells you nothing, then look at it this way: You just got a big head start on looking for a new job where you *can* get ahead.

> **Five more ways in which you can demonstrate to your boss that you have your shit together**
>
> Following instructions
> Owning up to your mistakes
> Being proactive
> Displaying this book on your desk
> Not being an insufferable prick

Fortunately, you have your shit together (and you added that accolade to your CV), so getting one shouldn't be a problem.

I'll show you my out-of-office if you show me yours

Once you've shored up your promotion and worked yourself into the ground to prove you deserved it, you get to take a much-deserved vacation. In part II, we saved up for it. Now you have to make sure you can get out the door to enjoy it, which often means cramming an extra week's worth of work into the five days before you depart. Score!

In this situation, consider **anticipation vs. reality,** and act accordingly.

By that I mean, the *anticipation* of leaving work behind—and all of the what-ifs and unknowns that come with that territory—is enough to send most people to the panic room. I used to freak the fuck OUT when I was getting ready to go on vacation—not only about getting an additional week's worth of my own work done, but about what other people might need from me while I was away — and then overprepare accordingly. Plus, I was always checking my goddamn email from vacation anyway, defeating the purpose of having pre-worried about things that might or might not even come up.

This whole rigmarole was **a master class in both anxiety and inefficiency.**

In *reality,* however, arriving back at the office after seven days aboard an all-inclusive Mediterranean cruise is what it is. You stay two hours late one night, power through a few hundred emails (seventy-five of which are immediately delete- or file-able, BTW), and go home to polish off the bottle of ouzo you bought at duty-free. First day back sucks, but you're relaxed and tanned. If you're Alvin, you're still drunk. You'll survive.

It took me until February of 2014 — a full fourteen years into my adult working life — to go away for more than a weekend without checking my work email. (Before we all had BlackBerrys, I checked work email on my honeymoon from the hotel "Business Centre." Remember those?) Coincidentally, my first email-free vacation was also my first-ever trip to the town in the Dominican Republic that I now call home, so it seems that keeping my mind clear of work really left room for that whole "living the dream" goal to take root. And I got through almost the entire 300-email backlog while waiting for a taxi home from JFK. That airport has notoriously long lines, but still.

My point is that **vacation overprep bleeds right into vacation work-doing,** and you need to nip that shit in the bud so you can enjoy the time off you so scrupulously scrimped and saved for. Not to mention, people who check their work email on vacation are 87 per cent more likely to drop their phones in a body of water, which adds one more thing to the to-do list upon return.*

Make like Elsa and let it go

If you're like me (or rather, Old Me), you prepare for vacation the week before you leave by doing all of your work, plus all the work for the week you'll be gone, and then you scurry around trying to half-finish tasks that aren't

---

* I made that up — but it sounds believable, doesn't it?

even on anyone else's radar yet, just *in case* they pop up before you get back. That last part takes "being responsible" to the level that bleeding ulcers are made of.

Listen to New Me: **Your job is to get *your* shit together, not worry about everyone else's.**

Letting go of things you can't control is a huge part of the mental decluttering process. And you definitely cannot control whether somebody else decides to do a certain part of *their* job one day while you're on vacation, and discovers that they need you for it.

Should you leave all of your responsibilities in a smouldering shit-heap while you swallow a fistful of peyote and commune with the giant saguaro at Big Willy's Dude Ranch? Of course not. But you also don't have to pre-do a bunch of stuff that might never come up. Pack that impulse up in a nice cardboard box and leave it on the street with a sign that says FREE SHIT. Somebody else will take it. Just like somebody else in your office will step in and get the ball rolling on the Q4 numbers if they really have to.

Or more likely, they'll just wait for you to get back. In which case you can **deal solely with the *reality*** of returning from vacation — **rather than adding *anticipation*** to your must-do list before you even leave.

Good things come to those who delegate

If not giving a fuck means no longer caring about/doing certain things, getting your shit together is about **making what you *need* to do easier and less stressful.**

Enter: delegating.

Because even better than deciding not to worry about things you can't control is making someone else worry about them instead, am I right? See ya later, delegator!

Delegating takes many forms, including:

If you have an assistant, you can assign a task to him because — hello — his job is to assist you. Easy.*

You can ask for help from a coworker, offering future coverage to them in return. A little quid pro quo goes a long way.

You can also take someone up on their *offer* to help

---

* And BTW, if keeping your house clean involves picking up toys, you can assign your child-assistants the task of doing that for themselves, saving yourself twenty minutes and five deep-knee bends. Delegating-as-teachable-moment!

you. If you're overloaded (whether before vacation or just every damn day), and someone — your assistant, your friend, your postman — notices and offers to take something off your plate, for the love of God say yes. And then say thank you.

Finally, you can step down from the starring role in your one-man version of *Oliver Twist*. All that "Please, sir, I want some more" is getting extremely tiresome, is it not? If you're in a meeting where assignments for additional work are being handed out like sugar-free lollipops at the dentist's office, I recommend not raising your hand. I vividly remember the last time I volunteered for extra work at my final corporate job and it led to one of the greatest failures/time-sucks of my professional life. **Sugar-free lollipops are *so* not worth it.**

Honestly, I don't know what it is about asking for more work that makes so many of us feel virtuous. **Stop asking for extra work!** Let other people who haven't read any of my books ask for it instead.

That's just good delegating.

But what if it doesn't get done to my standards?

Simon, Simon, Simon. We'll get to perfectionism in part IV, I promise. Part of delegating is not freaking out about *how* something gets done — just that it *gets* done, and not by you. Making life easier, remember? The worst thing that happens is the person you delegated to does a bad job, one or both of you cleans it up, and you move on.

If you're trading millions of dollars for a multinational corporation, you probably shouldn't have given Derek from Custodial Services your password and instructions to "just press the return key a few times a day and it'll be fine," but you'll have plenty of time to improve your delegating skills during your four-year fraud sentence. After all, in prison, getting somebody else to do your bidding is practically a spectator sport.

Nobody's going to die on the table

When it comes to protecting your time off — or your time in general — you need to **set boundaries and enforce them.** Once you've prepped, delegated, and traded in your cubicle for a cabana, you want to keep your mind clear of pesky work-related worries so you can enjoy your time off to the fullest. The single best way to do this is to **disconnect completely from your working life.** Not only should you resist the temptation to check email or call in, you shouldn't even leave that door open a tiny little bit in your out-of-office reply.

This is not disconnecting:

> *I'm currently taking my six precious vacation days of the year, but checking email periodically, and if your matter is urgent please call Jim, who will then hunt me down on my white-water rafting trip to get an answer for you two business days sooner than you would have got one otherwise.*

This is:

> *I'm currently on vacation and will respond to your message when I return.*

Unless you're a surgeon, nobody is going to die on the table because you were unreachable for six days. And I imagine if you are a surgeon, you probably didn't schedule a vacation during anyone's lung transplant, so go ahead and disconnect. You've earned it.

Taking the tension out of your pension

Has all this talk about vacations got you thinking about the *permanent* vacation? (Retirement. I mean retirement. Not death.) Then it's your lucky day, because I have all kinds of things to say about retirement!

Actually, no I don't. To be perfectly honest, there's nothing new to say about saving for retirement. It's genuinely astonishing to me how many people cannot get their shit together on this score, given how much excellent advice is available on the topic. What's the deal, guys?

I've already demonstrated (over and over again) how easy it can be to put away a little bit of money every day or every week in service to a larger goal—so assuming you have some change to spare, it shouldn't be the spare change that's holding you back.

I'm guessing **it's the time frame.**

Ironically, retirement — although it is probably the most important thing you'll ever save for — is a big, amorphous goal that feels less important the younger you are and then **really fucking important when you're too old to do anything about it.** Alvin (the chipmunk) has an excuse — he hasn't aged a day in fifty-five years. Alvins (the people) need to get their shit together and start working on this. No excuses.

If the distance between today and retirement seems too vast, and therefore the idea of saving for your twilight years lacks urgency, please consult the following charts to get an idea of what that time looks like in dollars and cents. **Compound interest — essentially, free money** — earns you interest on your initial investment PLUS interest on the accumulated value of your initial-investment-plus-interest, over and over, until you take it out of the market. It is a truly miraculous feat of arithmetic.

As I said, this isn't "new" information, but maybe my zesty presentation will strike a chord. I'll show you **your own investment, the amount you end up with at age sixty-five,** and **the return on investment,** aka the amount of money that just materializes in your account without you having to lift a finger.

You can also think of it as the amount that you're cheating your old, tired self out of if you don't start saving for retirement today.*

Check it out:

SAVINGS CHART #1
$1.00/DAY

	CONTRIBUTES (STARTING AT CURRENT AGE)	ENDS WITH (AT AGE 65)	RETURN (FREE MONEY!)
55	$3,650	$5,398	$1,748
50	$5,475	$9,817	$4,342
45	$7,300	$16,015	$8,715
40	$9,125	$24,707	$15,582
35	$10,950	$36,899	$25,949
30	$12,775	$53,999	$41,224
25	$14,600	$77,982	$63,382

* I used this online calculator, which accounts for a 7 per cent return and a 25 per cent tax rate in the US**: www.bankrate.com/calculators/retirement/traditional-ira-plan-calculator.aspx.

** These rates vary depending on where you are in the world—but wherever you are, compound interest is compound interest. Start watering that money tree and watch it grow and grow.

At $1/day (the price of a lottery ticket):

A 55-year-old would contribute $3,650 and wind up with $5,398 — **a return of $1,748**. Not too shabby, but it would have been nice to start sooner.

A 40-year-old would put $9,125 into his pension and have $24,707 in the account by the age of 65. That's **a return of $15,582**. I don't know about you, but I'm 38 and a $15,000 bonus for doing nothing sounds pretty sweet to me.

A 25-year-old would put $14,600 into her pension and have $77,982 in the account by the age of 65. She's the big winner with **an extra $63,382** to show for her timely commitment to retirement savings. SIXTY-THREE THOUSAND DOLLARS.

Now look what happens if you invest that $3.57* per day that we found back on page 127:

* The calculator only lets me use round numbers; you'd actually be contributing five cents more per year ($1,303.05 instead of the $1,303.00 I entered), therefore earning EVEN MORE MONEY than this chart shows.

SAVINGS CHART #2
$3.57 / DAY

	CONTRIBUTES (STARTING AT CURRENT AGE)	ENDS WITH (AT AGE 65)	RETURN (FREE MONEY!)
55	$13,030	$19,271	$6,241
50	$19,545	$35,046	$15,501
45	$26,060	$51,172	$25,112
40	$32,575	$88,204	$55,629
35	$39,090	$131,729	$92,639
30	$45,605	$192,774	$147,169
25	$52,120	$278,393	$226,273

At $3.57/day (the price of a collapsible shot glass key chain):

A 55-year-old would contribute $13,030 and wind up with $19,271 — **a return of $6,241.** That could buy a lot of early-bird dinners.

A 40-year-old would put $32,575 into his pension

and have $88,204 in the account by the age of 65 — **a return of $55,629.** Now we're talkin'.

A 25-year-old would put $52,120 into her pension and have $278,393 in the account by the age of 65 — **a return of $226,273.** I'm sensing a theme here.

Finally, what happens if you go for the big bucks?

SAVINGS CHART #3
$5.00/DAY

	CONTRIBUTES (STARTING AT CURRENT AGE)	ENDS WITH (AT AGE 65)	RETURN (FREE MONEY!)
55	$18,250	$26,990	$8,740
50	$27,375	$49,084	$21,709
45	$36,500	$80,073	$43,573
40	$45,625	$123,537	$77,912
35	$54,750	$184,496	$129,746
30	$63,875	$269,995	$206,120
25	$73,000	$389,912	$316,912

At $5/day (because it never hurts to round up):

A 55-year-old would contribute $18,250 and wind up with $26,990 — **a return of $8,740.**

A 40-year-old would put $45,625 into his pension and have $123,537 in the account by the age of 65 — **a return of $77,912,** which, by the way, is more free money over the course of 25 years than that dollar-a-day 25-year-old made in 40.

A 25-year-old would put $73,000 into her pension and have $389,912 in the account by the age of 65. That means she's *contributing* almost as much as she wound up with *total* on the dollar-a-day plan, and getting **a whopping $316,912 in return.** That is a certifiable shitload of dough.

I think I've made my point. Go ahead, I can wait while you set up your pension*.

---

* If you're employed and in the UK, you might not even have to lift a finger. By 2018, all employers must provide a workplace pension scheme. Yep, thanks to "automatic enrolment" you don't even have to remember to plant that money tree—in fact, you would have to actively choose *not* to water it by "opting out." And why would you, when your employer adds a sweet monthly contribution to your pension alongside the percentage of your salary from your paycheck? Now that's a no-brainer.

Health, Home & Lifestyle

Alright, don't get too excited about retirement just yet. First we need to get you there in one piece and with most of your organs in good working order. This section covers a range of diet and exercise tips that you may decide to ignore, but for what it's worth, I'll be taking some of my own advice and getting started on a long-procrastinated fitness regimen. Other things you could ignore include: the dirty dishes in your sink, the scum in your bathtub, and the fine patina of apathy on your floors. But if you feel like spending a bunch of time and energy cleaning your house, I'll explain how to maintain it—a trick you should probably master before attempting a large-scale home improvement project, which I'll also touch on. (Renovating the basement as a metaphor for renovating your life!) And finally, I will drop some knowledge with regard to being selfish—without being an asshole or an insufferable prick—on your way to winning at life.

Let's get physical

I've watched my fellow Americans trade treadmills for type 2 diabetes diagnoses for decades now, so I assumed most people feel like I do: I know I'm not terribly fit, but I don't really *care*. Which is why I was surprised that "Physical Health" ranked so high in my survey (second to "Work" and ahead of "Lifestyle") as an area in which people say they need help getting their shit together. Live and learn!

Me? I did all that shit in my teens and twenties, from "Buns of Steel" videotapes to six-mile runs on Sundays, and I hated every minute of it. I did it because I thought I had to, to be thin and consequently to feel good about myself. But my priorities changed over time, and just like you might be at peace with a messy bedroom, I'm at peace with a little extra jiggle in my wiggle if it means I don't have to spend another hour of my life sweating to the oldies ever again.

However, I have recently decided that I would like to be a little more limber. Maybe it's spending all day hunched over my laptop writing, or maybe it's just "being almost forty," but whatever the case, I'm starting to feel a touch stiff and creaky. So before this becomes a permanent condition, I'm going to do something about it.

Well, well, well, looks like I just set myself a goal. Now, to strategize...

First, I shall Google "stretching" to get an idea of what I could be doing to free my neck and back from the early-onset rigor mortis that currently holds them in its grip.

Next, I'll set aside some time for my new "must-do" item. Since I currently give myself an hour every morning to drink coffee and check my social media feeds, I think I can shave fifteen minutes off that lower-priority activity to free up room for stretching. (Note: I'm not just *adding* something to my day, time-wise. I'm fitting it in by **reducing time spent on a less important task.**)

Finally, tomorrow morning I'll wake up and do the deed. I'll let you know how it goes.

Work it out — or find the work-around

While stretching seems pretty easy (she said, before she ever tried it), other types of exercise will be more demanding, requiring longer focus and potentially hernia-inducing commitment. As I said, not my bag of stinky gym clothes, but it could very well be yours.

So the question is, **how important is it to you to make this whole physical fitness thing happen?** Sure, a few hundred people clicked a button on an anonymous survey, but they clicked that button because they haven't done anything about it yet. Why? Probably because the motivation hasn't *quite* caught up to them.

The Power of Negative Thinking can take you from an online survey to a kickboxing class.

Are you kinda sorta disgusted with yourself for being physically unfit? If the answer is no, then proceed to your fainting couch like the queen you are. If the answer is yes, then it's time to get your shit together. And if it's time to get your shit together, then you know where to start.

Gentlemen, set those goals!

If you actually like exercising, this goal shouldn't be too hard to achieve; you just need to *prioritize* it over two or three hours' worth of something else in your week that could be sacrificed to the gym. Watching Ab Roller infomercials in your sweatpants is not actual exercise.

If you don't like exercise that much, you have to weigh your distaste for squat-thrusts against your distaste for saddlebags. Negative thinking got you all fired up? Great, take that motivation to the mat! I'm the last person in the world who'd tell you that it's easy to run five miles a day or power through a power yoga class, but I'd be the first to tell you that committing to an exercise plan is ultimately a hell of a lot easier than wallowing in self-destructive behaviour and crippling depression. So there's that.

And if you hate exercising more than a *Scooby-Doo* villain hates those meddling kids and their stupid dog—but you're unhappy about how you look or feel—then maybe you need to get your shit together in a different area, to improve your health without sacrificing your *joie de vivre*.

I'm a big fan of not doing things you don't want to do (fact: I wrote a whole book about it), which means I'm also a big fan of **finding the work-around.** That could mean watching what you eat instead of watching your step count rise, or it could be exercising *while* doing something fun like, oh, I don't know, listening to an audiobook about not doing things you don't want to do?

Just an idea.

Get your sheets together

Chipmunks, if you take nothing else away from this book, you must understand that without the proper amount of sleep, your life is meaningless. Okay, maybe not *meaningless,* but significantly shittier. Like, a lot more shitty. Shitty Cent. Shitty Shitty Bang Bang. The Secret Life of Walter Shitty.

I'm serious. You need sleep and you need it regularly and you need to protect it like a mother lion protects her cubs. If you are ever — and I do mean *ever* — presented with the choice of sleep over accomplishing one last thing on your must-do list, you are hereby instructed to burrow down into that mattress like your life depends on it. Which it does.

Take the cinnamon bun, maybe leave the chocolate eclair

Regarding the other part of physical health — dieting — I have complicated feelings about that, which I'll touch upon in part IV. But **the concept of a good diet itself is not complicated.** As far as I'm concerned, it looks like this:

> Eat what you need to eat to function the way you need to function, don't overdo it if you want your heart and liver to *keep* functioning, and enjoy life while you're at it. Everything in moderation.

What? You didn't come here for low-cal smoothie recipes; you came here to get your shit together. I'm just calling 'em like I see 'em. Getting your shit together is all about being happy. Content. Not annoyed. Are you content and not annoyed when you're munching on your third pile of bean sprouts in one day like some fucking rabbit with a modelling contract?

Maybe you are. I don't know. Dieting makes me uncomfortable. Which means the only way I know how to help YOU do it is by whipping out my keys, phone, and wallet and getting GYST-theoretical with this shit.

Strategize: If you want to lose weight by eating less food, figure out how much less food you need to eat per day. SMALL, MANAGEABLE CHUNKS OF FOOD. Calorie counting is a very straightforward way to accomplish this. Half a can of BBQ Pringles (475 calories) oughta do it.

Focus: The time necessary to shed X pounds will depend on how many fewer calories you can realistically remove from your day without dying of malnutrition, plus some other shit like what kinds of foods those calories come from and whether you are also exercising (and what your metabolism is, but that's none of my business). Generally speaking, it takes 3,500 calories to maintain a pound of body weight, so if you can shave 500 calories/day off your current diet, you stand to lose a pound a week. Need to lose ten pounds? Give yourself ten weeks.

Commit: Don't eat the Pringles. Don't keep the Pringles in the house for

> Eating *healthily* is a whole other issue, and with apologies to my loyal fan base, it's not one I'm qualified to advise you on. My diet comprises 50 per cent pizza, 25 per cent red wine, 15 per cent "straight cheeses and liquor," and 10 per cent "things you can drink out of a pineapple."

anyone else. Don't walk down the Pringles aisle at the grocery store. Definitely do not marry a Pringles sales rep. Is your dog named Pringles? Get rid of your dog.

For most of us, losing weight is just maths + willpower. If you want it badly enough (see: The Power of Negative Thinking), you'll get it done. And you might relapse, and you might have to do it all over again, but there IS a way to do it. Eat less, move more.

Although, come to think of it, I hear weight loss is a $60-billion-a-year industry, and while self-help books with curse words in the title are a growing market, Pierre Dukan is outpacing me by a good $59.9999 billion.

Maybe I'm the one who needs to get my shit together?

Good clean living

While I spend some time contemplating how to turn my penchant for blaspheming into a billion-dollar global empire, you could spend some time contemplating what it takes to clean your house and actually keep it that way for more than three hours. Because there are some folks out there who claim it's possible to tidy once and remain tidy for life, but I have to say: I call bullshit.

At this point, **we're living in a post-tidying society.**

The "one-time deal" fantasy of tidying your home top to bottom is seductive, but it's not practical. Like having a threesome with your spouse and the beguiling older neighbour, you got what you wanted, but you still have to see each other in the hallway and walk on your rugs. The house is not going to let you off the hook after one go-round, and neither is the cougar in 3B.

Practically everyone I know (including me) has a story about dumping the contents of their kitchen cabinets onto the floor and bidding tearful goodbyes to a set of spatulas. That's great, it really is. But what happens when the narcotic haze of tidying lifts and Alvin decides to scram before he gets sucked into another round of Tupperware organizing?

I'll tell you what happens.

People get their tidying groove on for a few months, or even just a few weeks, and then...kinda lose the thread. The laundry stops migrating into the basket, the books and papers multiply like Kardashians in heat, the knick-knacks return with a vengeance. These folks spend so much time and energy clearing out their physical space, only to fill it back up again, with chaos and discount birdbaths.

Why is that?

Well, I submit that **if they'd had their shit together in the first place, the tidying bug would have stuck.** A flurry of physical tidying can be very effective in the short term, but it all goes to shit when you lack time and motivation to maintain it. *Mental* decluttering is the prerequisite for cleaning your house AND keeping it that way.

Yes, things are easier to keep clean if you start with a total purge (see: Inbox Zero), but you still have to work at it, if not every single day, then at least once or twice a week. Maybe less, if you live in a tiny house. In fact, the only reason to live in a tiny house is because you hate to clean. Tiny houses are an abomination. There, I said it. Moving on.

Does any of this sound familiar?

I need help decluttering and keeping it that way.

No matter what I do, my apartment is messy and gross. I'm incredibly envious of people for whom cleaning is a compulsion.

I have to spend several all-night sessions making my home presentable when my parents come to stay. I'd like it to be pretty much ready for visitors at all times.

For three of you it should sound very familiar, because these quotes are lifted directly from my survey responses. For the rest, if this is what your completely normal, non-*Hoarders* life looks like, then at least you know you're not alone by a long shot. You're also not helpless! If having a tidy house is top of your wish list, you can approach it just like everything else — by getting your shit together.

> **Goal:** Not only clean your house, but keep it clean for unexpected company, impromptu dinner parties, and your own general sanity.

> **Strategize:** Begin with a one-time clean-up. This doesn't have to be a life-changing magic-level purge, just one overall sweep that gets you to the "It'd be okay if the neighbours swung by" headspace. (Disregard the fact that neighbours don't just "swing by" any more; they text first.) Then divide your cleaning duties up by category, such as picking up toys, fold-

ing laundry, emptying the bins, or vacuuming, and pledge to tackle one or two at a time, every couple of days, for maintenance. No matter how much ground you have to cover, if you break it up into small, manageable chunks, it won't be so overwhelming.

Focus: Set aside time to complete each corresponding mini-goal. When you look at the small picture, you really only need twenty minutes for some of this shit. Toys go into boxes, shoes go into the closet, bins go out, and knick-knacks get righted (actually, just get rid of the knick-knacks). Twenty minutes every few days can go a long way to keeping the house ready for prime time, all the time. A task like vacuuming might take longer, but doing it once every two weeks for an hour is a lot easier than piling that hour of vacuuming on top of ten hours of other cleaning, isn't it?

Commit: If you've set your mini-goals, judged how long it takes you to complete them, then prioritized them into your must-do list, you'll have no more excuses for not keeping the house clean. You built the time into your day; now all you have to do is use it. You've effectively backed yourself into a corner with your own Henry hoover.

The fact is, you don't need to have a cleaning compulsion to maintain a tidy (or tiny) home. All you need to do is **make the work as easy as possible on yourself** — by breaking it into small, manageable chunks — and then it becomes part of your routine, just like watching the *Today* show or trimming your nose hair.

> I'm up to three days in a row on my stretching plan. At fifteen minutes per session per day, my neck already feels much better. Which means I accomplished for free in forty-five minutes what a chiropractor would charge about $150 for, *and* I neither had to leave my house, nor get dressed. #WINNING

In sum: Want a regularly clean house? Clean it regularly! Don't think you have time to do it? Prioritize it over things you want less. Still have too much on your to-do list? Whittle it down to the must-do.

And if you go through all these steps and you still find keeping a clean house impossible... **maybe it's time to admit that you don't really care?** I suspect that some people claim exasperation about the state of their cluttered countertops because they think they're *supposed* to want to be able to see the granite beneath the crumbs and months-old Christmas cards.

It's perfectly okay to admit that physical decluttering just isn't important to you.

That's the life-changing magic of not giving a fuck, and it truly lasts forever.

Changing Rooms is lying to you

If you do care about having a nice living space — and in fact you care so much about it that you want to **not only maintain, but *improve* your living space** — then having your shit together is the only way to fly. Any big, long-term project, of which home improvement is a positively *ripe* example, is just one giant goal broken up into a lot of smaller ones. Motivation and prioritizing are the first steps. Refinishing the dank, ugly basement has to become important enough to you that you finally give it a place of honour on your must-do list.

But must-do lists are typically all about *today* — or at

least a shortish period of time, right? (That was a rhetorical question. I know they are; I invented them.)

And a project like this could take weeks, months, or even years, depending on how much time, energy, and/or money you have to devote to it. So it may be "must-do" in terms of your priorities (you want to send the kids to that basement and get them out of your hair several years before sending them off to university accomplishes the same goal), but it's not going to happen all at once, in one day.

You know what *can* happen in one day?

A small, manageable chunk.

Zing!

Getting your shit together for the big stuff is just getting your shit together for a bunch of small stuff, over time. Of *course* a full renovation is daunting. Your basement is not going to magically transform itself all at once into a wall-to-wall-carpeted wonderland. There are, like, eight thousand things that have to get done to take a space from "unfinished concrete cell" to "tricked-out rec room." But it's just like we discussed on page 42 about getting a new job — all you need to do is strategize, focus, and commit. Keys, phone, wallet.

Yes, Alvin, it will require decisions and effort on your part, for a prolonged period of time. But crossing *one thing at a time* off the basement renovation must-do list is a relatively easy way to get there. Definitely easier than trying to do it all at once. Even those teams of contractors and designers on *Changing Rooms* actually take weeks to renovate a house. That whole "WE HAVE TWENTY-FOUR HOURS TO FLIP THIS PUPPY" is just for TV. Sorry if I burst your bubble there, but the truth will set you free.

Your chunks could look like this. So small, so manageable:

Decide to renovate basement

Research contractors

Pick a contractor

Make an appointment with your contractor

Choose paint colour

Choose light fixtures

Start thinking about light switch covers

Realize you don't give a shit about light switch covers

Instruct your contractor to select light switch covers him/herself

Let the contractor do his/her thing for a couple of weeks

Meanwhile, research couches, coffee tables, and media cabinets

Send strongly worded email to contractor about his/her lack of progress

Buy a cute throw pillow

Throw it at your contractor

Etc.

If you need to save up for your renovation (and I'm guessing you do, because who has that kind of cash lying around?), you already know how to do that, too. You could even be doing it *while* you research contractors.

If you don't intend to use a contractor — whether

you're on a budget, or you just enjoy doing this kind of thing yourself—the steps are largely the same. Cross off "research contractors," "pick a contractor," and "make an appointment with your contractor." Replace those with "paint the basement" and "install wall sconces."

And if you have neither the budget for a contractor nor the time/desire to do it all yourself, you may have to juggle that priority list some more and see what shakes out.

> **As to money and effort:** Maybe instead of extra bells and whistles you compromise by painting the room yourself—but cough up for a professional electrician (and wait to put the pool table in until after the kids leave home, so they can't ruin it).

> **If it's a time thing:** Perhaps watching eight hours of football every weekend could be sacrificed to building the perfect man cave over a period of several months. That's a lot of free kicks you could be putting toward a higher-priority *goal*. Haha, football puns! I slay me.

And now, I return to **motivation and priorities**: Is this shit worth it to you or not?

If not, go ahead and cross "basement renovation" off your list entirely. Whatever, no skin off my teeth. I don't even have a basement.

I've got a guy for that (and so could you)

We've already learned that sometimes the best way to do something is not to do it at all — i.e., let it go. Delegating it to someone else is even better. The thing gets done, and YOU didn't have to do it! Awesome.

But behind door number 3 is yet another option, the highest form of delegating, known as: **Hire a professional**.

Whether you're staring down the barrel of a small-scale repair, or a large-scale renovation, or just need your pants to be two inches shorter, going with a pro is another option for decluttering your mind and defusing the ticking time bomb that is your to-do list.

Yes, it costs money. But it frees up your valuable time

and energy. (And it ensures that those khaki slacks don't wind up full-blown capris. Someone whose paying job it is to hem pants usually gets it right on the first try.)

Sometimes getting your shit together is about admitting you DON'T have your shit together in a particular area.

It's about getting out of your own way so the world can move forward around you and you can stop wasting your time and energy on futile pursuits, like hemming pants or, say, fixing your own washing machine. Are you a washing machine repairman by trade? No? Then what are you doing back there? Oh, wasting a bunch of time and energy. Right.

Now, I'm not saying you have to be a washing machine repairman to have your shit together. But if you don't know jack shit about repairing washing machines yet you persist in putting "fix washing machine" on your must-do list and it never gets done, or gets done once and then the machine breaks again because you didn't really know what you were doing and therefore have to put "fix washing machine" *back* on the list—well, that's when you have to look yourself in the mirror and admit you don't have your shit together.

Please, do yourself (and your washing machine) a favour: Call the plumber and call it a day.

Winning by osmosis

When you're in the hands of someone who has their shit together, you feel safe and secure. Like a limping marathoner helped across the finish line by a fellow runner, so can you be buoyed by the indomitable spirit and skill of a professional plumber.

Hiring a pro can also be a *means* to an end, rather than the end itself.

It may be the best way to bridge the gap between the shit you do have together, and the shit you don't. For example, let's say you need a new phone, but you're so flummoxed by the various models constantly coming on the market that you've resigned yourself to talking into the tin-can-on-a-string you've had since before *Scrubs* was cancelled. In order to narrow your options, you could at least **consult a professional as a small, manageable step toward realizing your overall goal** (of choosing the phone that's right for you). It doesn't even cost you anything to walk into the Apple store armed with questions, and those nerds at the Genius Bar love talking battery life and megapixels. You'd be doing *them* a service.

Finally, if you can afford it, hiring a professional is just easier.

If you're lucky enough to have the means to keep someone else's business afloat, throw 'em a bone! The goal here is getting through life with minimal hassle and maximal gain. You know you've truly got your shit together when you have time to relax and enjoy a turkey sandwich — not when you're filling every moment of every day with unnecessary aggravation.

SHIT YOU COULD HIRE A PROFESSIONAL TO DO, SAVING YOURSELF THE AGGRAVATION	SHIT YOU COULD DO INSTEAD
Wash your car	→ Clean the gutters
Clean the gutters	→ Mow the lawn
Mow the lawn	→ Paint the deck
Paint the deck	→ Make some lunch
Make some lunch	→ Wash your car

See what I did there?

In a world where you have **one too many things on your plate,** paying somebody else to do that one extra thing for you could be **the key to getting everything *else* accomplished**. It releases a chunk of time and energy, even if it means sacrificing some money to the overall cause.

This is a particularly good strategy for people who can afford the help but inexplicably refuse to ask for it while projects pile up around them like the ruins of so many ancient Roman civilizations. Take that must-do list of yours and see what you can pawn off on someone else — for free, for a case of beer, or for twenty bucks an hour.

Get your shit together. Divide and conquer. It worked for Caesar.

PS Don't be such a fucking martyr

I like a good whinge as much as the next gal, but for God's sake nobody needs to hear about how busy you are every hour of every fucking day. A pity party is a shitty party. And more importantly, you should not *be* busy every hour of every day. Winning life is supposed to make you feel freer and looser,

---

like so many pairs of linen pants. It's not a competition—
with yourself or anyone else—to be the most booked up,
burdened, and burnt out. I mean, look what happened to
Joan of Arc. SHE WAS A MARTYR AND SHE WAS
LITERALLY BURNT OUT.

"Me time" is a right, not a privilege

Boy, now we're really cooking, aren't we? (Sorry, Joan.) I
think it's time to move on from all the shit that *needs* to
get done, and start talking about the shit we simply *want*
to do. Because for many of us, it's difficult to justify making time for such activities—aka "hobbies"—that seem
to benefit no one but ourselves.

Fuck. That. Shit.

Sacrificing your hobbies to the altar of the must-do list
is no good. They should be ON the must-do list to begin
with. **This book is all about decluttering your mind and
training yourself to think differently about your life and
how you live it.** "You do you" with instructions on *how* to
do you, for maximum happiness. So instead of relegating

crossword puzzles and cross-country skiing to the "some-day when I have time" corner of your brain, make room for them right up front. Easy access.

To do this, you have to consider your hobbies — and the benefits you get from indulging in them — **to be as important as the other stuff you "need" to do.** You *need* to get up and go to work, because you *need* to make money to live on. But you also *need* to NOT be sad and NOT be frazzled and NOT be marinating in a cauldron of resent-ment 24/7, right?

What makes you not sad, frazzled, and resentful? Why, blowing off a little steam at the Go-Kart track, of course. Or pottering in the garden or going salsa dancing or zon-ing out to Elvis Costello while you perfect your latest batch of mead. Hobbies are not only an integral part of maintaining your happiness, they can go a long way toward balancing the annoyance of the more arduous, less exciting must-do tasks on your list. You can think of time spent on a hobby as a reward for

Hobbies with which I have rewarded myself for getting other shit done

Reading a book
Sunbathing
Counting lizards
Going for a brisk walk
Taking a bubble bath

completing annoying, time-and-energy-sucking shit. (And a hobby doesn't have to be all that high-energy itself — it can be merely a distracting or restorative pastime: See sidebar.)

If you need any more convincing, I can tell you that I spent a great deal of my insurance company's money on anxiety doctors in the early 2010s and I was told by MEDICAL PROFESSIONALS that I should take more bubble baths. Not because bubble baths themselves are fucking delightful, but because one way to "down-regulate" (fancy term for calm yo'self) is to **switch your focus** from The Thing That's Causing Your Anxiety to A Thing That Makes You Happy. It's like tricking your brain into feeling better.

But what if my brain resists such trickery? My brain is no fool. My brain is a force to be reckoned with!

Then reckon with it.

You have to lobby for your hobby

As someone with a perennially Pisa-esque tower of books on my nightstand, I often have to remind myself that reading is a worthy pastime — even if I *could* be doing something more "useful" with my afternoon, like generating my quarterly expense report. Yet I've never been sorry about winning that mental argument for pleasure reading; whereas guilting myself into a *pas de deux* with QuickBooks results in language emanating from my mouth that wouldn't be out of place at a Brooklyn Navy Yard bar circa 1941.

Whether your diversion of choice is reading, fly-fishing, or ripping a massive bong hit and then trying to solve a Rubik's Cube, you need to **treat it like a lobbyist treats his or her cause,** advocating for and influencing the government's decision favourably toward it. Fortunately, you are both the lobbyist and the legislator in this scenario, so you have a real inside track. You give a fuck about books, backcasting, and Blue Lightning Kush? Great, now ensure that these activities are well represented on your calendar. **Schedule them in.**

A highly effective way to increase time spent on a hobby is **to *let yourself* spend time on a hobby to *remind yourself* how much joy it brings.** Then when you're faced with that mental debate about smoking up vs. buckling down, your inner lobbyist won't have to work so hard to persuade the government that you have a right to your 10:00 PM date with Chandler T. Bong.

Finally, when in doubt: Don't think. *Do.*

Don't even bother hemming and hawing and bargaining with your brain. Just do what I do — turn on the tap and climb on into the tub before you can second- (or third-) guess yourself out of it. Once you're there, your brain will readjust to all the positive vibes it gets from doing something you actually *want* to be doing, and you'll be happy about it.

That's some real chicken-and-egg shit, I know, but it works.

Becoming pro-creation

Lots of people who responded to my survey said they wished they could get their shit together to pursue not only hobbies, but specific creative goals — like writing, music, and art — but are too bogged down in work, family commitments, or other obligations of the no-fun variety.

I hear you loud and clear.

It's not easy to "make time" for stuff that doesn't [yet or

may never] pay the bills. But novels don't write themselves, guitars don't gently weep on command, and perfect Bakewell tarts aren't as easy as Mary Berry makes them look. At some point, you have to get your shit together in order to stop aspiring to do the thing and ACTUALLY DO THE THING, whether it pays bills or just makes you happy.

The path to this version of life-winning is obstructed by two separate but related challenges. We'll call them **the Scylla and Charybdis of getting your shit together.***

Scylla is **scheduling.** If you work all day and have a busy family/social life — or are just so tired you keel over when you get home — when do you have time for creative stuff?

Answer: You have to *make* or *find* time.

By now, you probably expect me to trot out my trusty must-do list. And yeah, that's one way to tackle it, but its efficacy **depends on the kind of creative person you are.** A former colleague of mine worked on her novel very early in the morning before going to her day job. Apparently

---

* I can't pronounce their names either, but they were mythical sea monsters that flanked the one safe path through the Strait of Messina in Homer's *Odyssey*. Just focus on the sea monster imagery and you'll be fine.

she was capable of producing quality words at this time every day—and committed to doing so regularly—because she ended up with a jillion-dollar book deal, and quit the day job.

A victory for must-do lists everywhere!

For others, the creative urge has to strike, and *then* you have to find time to exploit it. A melody might pop into your head during your morning commute, but you can't just bail on your 8:00 AM presentation because you suddenly found yourself in the groove. Still, you could take five minutes to jot down the basics of your inspiration and shuffle tomorrow's must-do list accordingly, to prioritize writing a new song. Not ideal, but it's a start. Scylla, you can work with.

This is where Charybdis comes in, which is **the mistaken idea that there is no value in the creative stuff** you're trying to schedule. Sailing safely around this salty sea-witch means accepting the notion that you may be devoting an hour—or several—every day or week to an activity that has no perfectly defined purpose, one that might result in a finished product or might not. Spending an afternoon painting in your room could be an extremely rewarding period of craft-honing that brings you a lot of joy even if it doesn't land you a gallery show. Then again, it might very well land you a gallery show just like it landed my former coworker a book deal. **You'll never know until you try, will you?**

Therefore, the best, most potentially winning path toward achieving your creative goals lies between **finding time *and* granting yourself permission to use it.** Tapdance right past Scylla and slip Charybdis a high five on your way.

Selfish is not a four-letter word

Whether you're taking time "away" from your kids to play mah-jongg with the girls, or taking time "away" from your wife to hang out alone in a darkroom for a few hours and get your Ansel Adams on, making room for hobbies and creative goals is **a prime example of my get-your-shit-together practice overlapping with my no-fucks-given philosophy.**

After *The Life-Changing Magic of Not Giving a Fuck* came out, I gave interviews where I talked about being selfish as a good thing, and some people viewed that as a controversial stance. I was accused both of contributing to the downfall of society and of being a millennial, neither of which is accurate and one of which is deeply offensive.

But none of that criticism has changed my mind in the slightest. I firmly believe that being selfish — in pursuit of your health and well-being — can be a good thing for you AND everyone in your life. If you're happy and fulfilled, that automatically makes you a better person to be around. A more relaxed parent. A kinder partner. A more patient boss and a more energetic employee. **You can't give of yourself to others if there's nothing left of yourself to give, can you?**

So yeah, giving fewer, better fucks is an exercise in selfishness — focusing on what you *want* to do rather than what you *need* to do (or what *other people* think you *should* do). But there's nothing wrong with that! And this mind-set serves you especially well in getting your shit together to pursue hobbies, creative work, or any other activity that doesn't necessarily "result" in anything other than you being happy.

I've got news for you: **Happiness is a goal in and of itself.**

A couple of years ago, when I was still mired in corporate drudgery and the white-sand beaches of Hispaniola were barely a twinkle in my eye, my parents were visiting us in New York, and we were seated around our dining table shooting the shit.

We were talking about my husband and me not having kids, and how some people of my parents' generation don't understand that particular life choice. I mused aloud about how, if we were to breed, I would just end up being Bad Cop to his Good, especially because I knew I wouldn't be able to stop riding my kids' asses to be "successful."

"Even if I *tried* to take it easy on them, I'd just keep thinking about how I did all my schoolwork and graduated at the top of my class and got into a good university and have this great career because I worked so hard — instead of this guy [gestures to husband] who was focused on mere happiness his entire life!"

That's when my parents looked at me, horrified, and my husband (who's pretty fucking successful, I might add) kind of patted me gently on the arm.

"Whoa," he said.

"*Mere* happiness?" they said.*

---

* My parents were not hard on me as a kid. I was hard enough on myself for all of us, trust me.

That conversation was what we in the biz term a "wake-up call." Except it was more like staying at the Marriott on Bourbon Street and asking them to provide a 6:00 AM brass band on your balcony, extra trombone.

No surprise that the quit-my-job-and-move-to-the-Caribbean plan was enacted soon after that, is it? I had my goal. It was time to strategize, focus, and commit.

How about you, Alvin? Is it time yet?

IV

DEEP SHIT:
Mental health, existential crises, and making big life changes

As I wrote this book, I realized maybe I'm not a straight-up Simon after all, but more of a Simon with my moon in Theodore. I can admit that when shit gets totally overwhelming, I occasionally give in to temptation to hide under my bed for a day or three. (Hey, keeping your shit together is a constant undertaking, even for a type-A neurotic who eats Post-it notes for breakfast.)

But when I have a "Theodore Moment," I try to relax, take my own advice, and remember all the truths I hold to be self-evident: Strategize, focus, commit. Prioritize and delegate. When in doubt, hire a pro. And try to do it all without losing my mind.

Still, there's a decent amount of mental clutter — **like anxiety and perfectionism** — that will always be hanging out in my brain and which necessitates vigilant, regular tidying. For other people, that clutter could be a penchant for **avoidance and self-sabotage,** or a **crippling fear of failure.** Basically, if the Game of Life is one big race around the track, these are the psychological hurdles that we put up in our own lanes (especially Simons, but no chipmunk is immune).

Part IV is all about this **deep shit**. Real **bottom-of-the-rut, scraping-it-off-your-shoes-for-days kind of stuff.**

And the sooner you dive on in, the faster you can climb on out.

Getting your shit together to get out of your own way

First things first: Maintaining your mental health and solving existential crises are just like getting your shit together to go on a diet or paint your apartment. You know twenty-four pounds doesn't melt away in twenty-four hours, and that before you can paint, you have to move furniture and put down drop cloths and tape the baseboards. Well, anxiety doesn't get cured in one wave of the magic feather duster, nor does fear of failure succumb to the Mr. Clean Magic Eraser in *just five minutes!!!*

Like everything else we've covered so far, **life's deepest shit gets tidied up and swept away one small, manageable chunk at a time.**

When I talk about "getting in your own way," I'm talking about that deep shit. Not your sub-par time management and delegating skills, but your emotions and your attitude. Your *mentality* itself. **This clutter takes the form of mental dust**—it's largely invisible but always there, and the longer you ignore it, the more invasive it becomes. It covers all the REST of your clutter with a layer of extra shit and seeps into the cracks and crevices, calling for a slightly more finessed approach to mental tidying. We're still using the tried-and-true combo of strategy, focus, and commitment, but it's **actually happening inside you,** as opposed to on the mat at the gym or high atop a ladder in your guest room.

To that end, the following pages contain advice of the kind you might also want to seek from, oh, say, a doctor or licensed counsellor. Of which I am neither, so please take everything I say with a grain of salt.* Pink Himalayan sea salt if you're feeling frisky.

Anxiety, you ignorant slut

Remember when I said we all have our *Oh shit* moments? Well, sometimes I have mine topped with bacon, cheese, and a nervous breakdown. It doesn't happen nearly as

---

* I imagine that if you bought a book with the word *shit* in the title, you were already prepared to do this, but I'm sure my publisher would prefer that all of our asses remain suitably covered. Thank you.

often as it used to, but when it does, that cloud of mental dust isn't going anywhere until I start sucking it up. (Alvins and Theodores have a little buildup in the corners, but we Simons have been vacuuming this shit up and then inexplicably dumping the filter right back onto the floor our entire lives. It's a problem.)

Giving fewer fucks goes some way toward solving this problem—you'd be amazed how many layers of anxiety-dust you can clear out when you **stop caring about what other people think of your life choices.** But you still have to *live* your life, and that means dealing with stuff that occasionally leaves you feeling like you're making out with a Roomba.

Barring pharmaceutical intervention (which again, I'm not licensed to prescribe, though I heartily endorse it), here are three simple approaches that could work for you.

Ripping off the Band-Aid

This is useful in situations where you literally cannot move forward without taking action. For example, if getting your shit together means moving out on your roommate and into your own place where there are no takeout containers being used as ashtrays or guys named Clint buzzing at all hours, you may feel some anxiety about telling your bestie that you're breaking the lease, but you do *have* to tell her. You can't just pull a disappearing act in the middle of the night and you certainly can't pay double rent to maintain a second apartment just so you never have to talk turkey. Just do it. The anxiety you feel beforehand will be 1,000 per cent mitigated by the relief you feel after, in your smoke-free, Clint-free one-bedroom.

This Too Shall Pass

The opposite of the Band-Aid approach, this is when you ignore the problem juuuuuust long enough that it resolves itself or goes away. I'm not talking full-scale avoidance — a bad habit I'll address in a moment — but a few deep breaths' worth of prudent hesitation; maybe a day at most.

Say you get a cryptic email from your boss that sends you into panic mode. It's probably wise not to respond right away. Focus on something else for a while and it's entirely possible that with a little distance, you'll reread the message and it will reveal itself as totally innocuous. Or your boss will poke her head into your office and say something nice and you'll realize you were reading way too deeply into *Come see me when you have a second. Thanks.*

The Practice Test

Does anxiety sometimes manifest itself as having a never-ending conversation in your head instead of having that conversation with the real person who's causing you the anxiety? If so, I recommend getting it down on paper. This is a proven-effective therapeutic method and it's also fun to write sentences like *You are literally the worst person I've ever met in my life, and if I could, I would find out where you live, wait until winter, sneak into your house, and leave a McDonald's Filet-O-Fish sandwich tucked under your radiator. But since I don't have time for that shit, let me just say that what you did at SoulCycle last Friday was unforgivable and you should be ashamed of yourself, Nancy.*

The act of writing this stuff down helps release your anxiety into the void, and often prevents you from ever needing to *have* a real-life confrontation. If I predecease him, my husband has explicit instructions to burn my collection of yellow legal pads.*

Avoidance is not a zero-sum game

We want to limit the amount of panic-inducing anxiety you experience, yes, but we can't let you go all catatonic. Staring blankly at your to-do list does not cause the items on it to migrate dutifully off the page like a herd of goddamn lemmings. If you abuse "This Too Shall Pass" (more of an issue for Alvin and Theodore; Simons' anxiety tends

---

* They tell you to do it longhand, which is the part that scientifically helps reduce anxiety. But that also means you can't accidentally *send* your furious jottings to anyone. It's easy to activate Gmail in a fit of pique. It's not easy to send anything via Royal Mail, let alone do it accidentally.

to manifest in being *reactive* rather than *inactive*), you may think you're getting away with something, but you're actually adding to your overall burden:

Avoiding doing laundry leaves you with no underwear

Avoiding taking out the bins makes your kitchen smell like rancid chicken

Avoiding uncomfortable conversations delays resolution

I'm going to unpack that last one a little bit, since it's a gateway to all sorts of problems — like anxiety, stomach pain, and sleepless nights — whereas the overflowing basket/bin is just a gateway to going commando/rats.

Like confronting the Wizard of Impulse Control, you sometimes — perhaps even often — have to confront real, live humans about annoying shit in order to get things done. You may be a boss who has to reprimand an employee, or an employee who has to defy a boss. You may be a spouse or partner who has beef with your spouse or partner. You may need to ask your mother, once and for all, to stop meddling in your life.*

Whatever the case, it's much better to get your shit together and do it, before the **Black Cloud of Confrontation** takes up permanent residence in your brain, shadowing all your other needs, desires, and obligations with its menacing gloom.

Fortunately, difficult confrontations operate on the same

> ### How to start a difficult conversation
>
> Make an appointment (nobody likes an ambush)
> Practise non-threatening hand gestures
> Open your mouth
> Use your words
> Try not to spit on anyone

principle of **anticipation vs. reality** that we discussed re: vacation prep on page 170. Half the battle is in the anticipation, so the sooner you strategize, focus, and commit to having "The Talk," the sooner you're into the backstretch of reality, and then all of a sudden it's over and it wasn't as bad as you *anticipated* it would be.

---

* This is in no way directed at my mother, who has made a very successful career of "not meddling in my life."

Of course, joy-related anticipation is one thing, while annoy-related anticipation is quite another. By all means, anticipate your little heart out when it comes to the build-up of excitement around the festival season, birthday parties, and the *Hamilton* Christmas album.* Milk that shit for all it's worth. But anticipation of annoying tasks is a real buzzkill, and avoidance only gives it room to fester.

Festering is a gross word. You shouldn't let things fester.

The other F-word(s)

Okay, so I may be the only one with a thing against *fester*, but I bet when you were a kid, you weren't supposed to say *fuck* in front of your parents, right? (Or, according to some Amazon reviewers, use it as an adult 732 times in one book.) And you were probably also not supposed to bring home a test or a report card bearing a big red F as a symbol of your poor grasp of trigonometry or inability to

---

* As far as I know this isn't a real thing, but it might be, after some enterprising producer reads this book.

memorize pertinent details of wars that were fought two hundred years before you were born.

That F was for FAILURE, and it struck another F-word—FEAR—into the hearts of schoolchildren everywhere. Forget about your own level of personal integrity for a moment: Would an F lose you TV privileges? Would your allowance be withheld? Would you be forced—*the horror*—to attend summer school?

Unacceptable! (And I'm sure there were much worse consequences/punishments depending on what kind of school you went to or what kind of parents you had.)

Well, it's no surprise that kids who were brought up under a constant threat of failure might internalize it a step too far. Some of them (about half, according to my survey) become adults for whom the teacher's scrawl has morphed into **a proverbial scarlet letter.** Fictional Puritan minx Hester Prynne had to sew an A for *adulteress* on all of her clothes. These peeps are staring down a big red F—not on their report cards, but emblazoned on their chests—branding them for life as FAILURES if they don't stay seventeen steps ahead at all times.

Eventually the *fear* of failure **becomes just as powerful and punishing as the failure itself,** and it can be crippling. (Not to mention ruin a lot of perfectly good shirts.) By being afraid of a *potential* bad outcome, you cause yourself even more agony surrounding the whole endeavour — whether it's passing a test, getting a promotion, or correctly assembling any piece of IKEA furniture on the first try.

The resulting **mental röran*** leads to…

Analysis paralysis

Have you ever worked with or for someone who just couldn't make a decision to save their ever-loving soul?

I once had a coworker whose **to-do list was composed entirely of avoidance.** Avoid approving that marketing plan. Avoid signing off on that copy. Avoid responding to those emails. This woman emphatically did not have her shit together and she — and everyone around her — suffered accordingly.

Her problem was not perfectionism (a battle all its own, which I'll discuss in the next section); perfectionists

---

* That's IKEA for "clutter."

tend to do, and redo, and re-redo things as opposed to never doing them at all.

It wasn't lack of understanding about what the job required; she'd been in the industry for a long time and was super-smart.

It wasn't even a personality thing; she was charming and lovely when she wanted to be — she just never "wanted to be" returning your calls.

No, I think her inability to make a decision — to either **focus** or **commit** — was about fear. Maybe she feared being reprimanded (although she may have been bringing more ire down upon herself by not doing *anything* than she would have by doing some things poorly). Maybe she feared getting fired if she made *too many* bad decisions in a row—but of course, you have to make one to get to the whole "in a row" part.

Whatever the case, **her strategy — avoidance — was shit.**

And ultimately, fearing things to the point of paralysis seemed to catch up to her — in addition to being on the arse-end of many irate voice mails, she *eventually did get fired*. Not winning.

The call is coming from inside the house

Not having your shit together is self-sabotage, pure and simple. You lost track of your keys, phone, and wallet? Great. You're locked out, blacked out, and tapped out. Do the same with your metaphorical shit and you're likely to lose even more: opportunities, friends, respect, and the Game of Life altogether.

A lot of people allow fear to put them on the defensive. As a result, they lose sight of their goal and the path it takes to get there. Strategy flies out the window. The focus switches to "everyone else" instead of "me." And the only commitment they can muster is in making excuses for their behaviour instead of changing it.

But in most cases? The world is not out to get you. YOU are out to get you. To paraphrase the Beastie Boys: You're scheming on a thing that's a mirage, and I'm trying to tell you now, it's self-sabotage.

As Frankin D. Roosevelt once said, "The only thing we have to fear is fear itself." I would add unruly dogs, skydiving, and cancer to the mix, though I do not personally fear failure. But for everyone who does, as I said on page 176, there are very few situations in which anyone is going to die on the table because you made the wrong decision. It doesn't have to be so fear-inducing.

And if you're just a regular person with regular decisions to make, I'd wager that none of them are *so* critical that they should keep you up at night at your virtual sewing machine embroidering virtual Fs onto all your polos.

Instead, I suggest sewing yourself an *A*—not for *adulteress*, but for *acceptance!*

When you **accept that failure *is* an option**, you move it from the realm of anxiety-inducing anticipation into a reality that you'll deal with when (and more importantly, IF) it ever happens. Your energy is better spent on accomplishing goals in the here and now than on worrying about failure in the abstract. And if you do fail, it's not the end of the world—unless you were supposed to warn us about that world-destroying asteroid I mentioned on page 64.

Failure is just a thing that happens. Sometimes you bring it on yourself, like when you go to Burning Man without adequate sunscreen and Wet Wipes. Other times, it just sort of happens to you, like when you took a degree in astronomy

> **Things that are healthier to fear than failure**
>
> Sharks
> Bandits
> Scaffolding
> Poisonous toads
> A Republican-controlled
>   Congress
> Third nipples

without knowing Asteroid 4179 Toutatis was going to collide with the planet on your watch. You can't win 'em all.

In other words: In order to get your shit together, you need to **stop giving a fuck about failure.** Which is an excellent use of F-words, if I do say so myself.

Just say no to being perfect

If avoidance and fear of failure are applicable across the chipmunk board,* perfectionism is, I think, more common in Simons. There are some especially nitpicky Alvins out there, but frankly, they should be prioritizing "doing stuff" before they get to "doing it perfectly," *n'est-ce pas?*

To Simons, perfection is a bright, shining beacon toward which they must march with hunger and purpose if they really want to win at life. But in fact, perfection is an illusion, a shimmering oasis in the desert of their

---

* Now I'm picturing a boardroom full of chipmunks, which is really cute.

minds. Like trying to diet your way to Kate Upton, **holding perfection in your sights is a self-defeating strategy.**

Which is why I'm here today to tell you:

My name is Sarah, and **I am a recovering perfectionist.**

Yes, it's true. I'm a grade-A tweaker, constantly fighting the urge to redo the same shit over and over until it's PERFECT. This unhealthy behaviour will always be part of me, and each day is a battle against giving in to it.

Sound familiar? If so, consider the variety of things you might have to accomplish on any given day:

Write a memo for your boss

Pick up your dry cleaning

Design a baby shower invite for your friend, clean your apartment for your parents' impending visit, and make a reservation at your dad's favourite seafood joint (the man loves a nice piece of fish)

Now, let's say it took you most of the day, but you finished the memo. You lost at least an hour deleting and reinstating semicolons, but that's par for the course, right? Everybody does that! (No, they don't.)

You got your delicates out of hock just before your dry cleaner flipped the CLOSED sign in the window, but that meant you had to lug a garment bag around while you canvassed three different stationery stores for paper for the shower invite. The first two shops had blue, but not the "Superman's tights" hue you had your heart set on. You finally found *that,* ran home, shoved a taco in your face, and then started hunting for fonts.

Ooh, that's a good one. But what if there's a way to sans-serif the first letter of each line and then small-caps the time and date, and use the script version of that other font for the ampersands because when they're ever so slightly tilted they look like little storks and . . .

Oh, hey, can't stop tweaking, can you? Yep, join the club.

Tweak.

At a certain point, the time and energy you've poured into any of the items on your must-do list is going to reach **critical mass,** and the more of it you spend trying to get one thing *perfectly* perfect, the less time you have for any of the rest. Suddenly — despite your best intentions — **instead of having your shit together, your whole day has gone to shit.** It's too late to vacuum or your downstairs neighbour will complain, and Barnacle Billy's just gave away their last table for Saturday night. At this rate, your mum will be bleaching your toilet while your dad eats microwaved Captain Birdseye, and you'll probably spill tartare sauce on your freshly dry-cleaned blouse, just for good measure.

Tell me, Simon. Have you ever heard the saying "Don't let the perfect be the enemy of the good?" Well, in our case, **we can't let the perfect be the enemy of the win.**

Think about it for a minute. **Even the biggest, most celebrated winners are rarely actually perfect.** A competitive gymnast may be *aiming* for a fabled "perfect ten," but that almost never happens (especially with this new scoring system, which seems designed to drive little leotarded Simons to drink vodka shooters off the balance beam).

And if one of those human pogo sticks can win an *Olympic gold medal* without being perfect, then you can certainly win at your own motherfucking life.

I'm telling you, kids, don't get hooked on perfection. It's no way to live.

Twelve steps for defeating perfectionism

1. Admit that, unlike the 1972 Miami Dolphins, you are powerless over perfection.
2. Believe that a power greater than you can help restore you to sanity.
3. Make a decision to turn your will over to the care of a lady who curses a lot.
4. Take a fearless inventory of your to-do list and then ruthlessly reduce it to a must-do list. Then go get some ice cream.
5. Confess to the exact nature of your perfectionism — but don't be too exact.
6. Be entirely ready to almost banish perfectionism from your life.
7. Humbly inquire of someone else whether you are, in fact, being ridiculous.
8. Make a list of all persons harmed by your perfectionist tendencies and be willing to apologize for being such a fucking stickler.
9. Make direct amends, except when you were totally right to be a stickler because otherwise your team never would have won the International Sand Sculpting Championships in Virginia Beach last year.
10. Continue to take inventory of your actions and make a mental note each time the world does not end because you failed to be perfect.
11. Improve your conscious understanding of giving fewer fucks and getting your shit together, referring as needed to the "bibles" in these fields.
12. Carry this message to other perfectionists; just don't be an insufferable prick about it.

Help wanted

By now, I hope all my chipmunks are feeling optimistic. That your capacity to get your shit together is inversely proportional to these dwindling pages, and you're running a white-gloved finger around that mental dust build-up like Mary fucking Poppins. Simons are probably working their twelve steps and then inventing new deep-breathing exercises because they just can't help themselves, but still. Progress.

We're almost ready to find out what the other side has to offer, but — and I want to be completely honest with you — we haven't quite hit rock bottom yet on the Deep Shit Ravine. For that, I've been preparing a special guided tour. I'm going to tell you about a time when I had to **get my shit together on an intensely deep psychological level** — one that made quitting my job and filling out a chart on my refrigerator look mighty shallow by comparison.

And I hope it will speak to any reader — Simon or otherwise — who's gone through something similar.

In order to tell this story properly I have to get a bit more serious, which means pressing Pause on the naughty puns and scatological humour for, like, four pages. Will you indulge me? I promise we'll be back to our regularly scheduled tomfoolery in no time.

Scout's honour.

The case of the disappearing girl

I was what you might call a chubby kid. I was also smart and funny and capable of memorizing "We Didn't Start the Fire" in its entirety, but my classmates mostly focused on the chubby thing. There was a lot of sniggering and at least one beach field trip that left permanent scars on my fragile young psyche. By the time secondary school rolled around, I wanted nothing more than to waltz into my first year with a new lease on life and new size-eight acid-washed Levi's.

So, like any budding Simon, I got motivated and got to work.

At thirteen years old, dieting via strict calorie control was the easiest thing in the world; my metabolism hadn't yet taken early retirement and the pounds melted away.

But obsessive calorie counting eventually (some might say "predictably") led me down the path to outright anorexia—a slowly peeled orange for lunch, dinner measured out in tiny increments of rice and chicken. In fact, I only ate dinner at all to keep up appearances around my family. If I could avoid ingesting food back then, I did.

You might say I had excellent willpower.

Eventually I was officially thin and confident about my body for the first time I could remember, but once an overachiever, always an overachiever. What if I could crack the code and return to enjoying tasty food in my mouth, but not gain back any weight? Brilliant! Surely I was the first person to think of swallowing dinner and then regurgitating it like a mama bird minus the hungry chicks.

Soon it was "Look at me, eating this cheeseburger. Nothing to see here, folks. Move along [while I throw it up in the bathroom or sometimes by the side of the road during my daily jog]." Graduating from anorexia to bulimia kept me skinny, but no matter how good I felt *about* my body, by this time my body itself felt pretty gross.

I had a sore throat, puffy eyes, and permanent cotton mouth. Because I wasn't actually digesting any nutrients,

I was anaemic, which meant I had to take nasty iron pills that caused me to burp uncontrollably all day. I'd transformed from a chubby kid into an emaciated 100-pound teen with a very attractive belching habit. (In a doubly *ironic* twist, the iron pills made me nauseous unless taken with food.)

But the gory details of an eating disorder aren't the point here. It's **how I found my way out of it** that I hope can help people with similar problems, as well as in a more general context.

Anyone who has endured self-harming behaviour of any kind will recognize the **feeling of *knowing* that what you're doing is unhealthy and untenable, but also feeling powerless to change it.** All day, every day, one *Oh shit* moment on top of another. Your brain becomes so cluttered, you can't even locate joy, let alone access it. It's buried real, real deep.

At sixteen years old, I didn't really understand the concept of hiring a professional to fix what was wrong with me, nor did I have the means to do so. But I knew I needed help. I decided my best chance to put a stop to my behaviour was to tell my mother what was going on with me — confess to my problem, and be held accountable to her, instead of to myself. It was the *Who Raised You?* strategy in its purest form.

The first small, manageable chunk of this plan would be saying the words: *I need help*.

I picked a night when we'd be alone in the house, sat down across from her on the living room couch, and spat those motherfuckers out. It was a scary, panicky moment of commitment, and then…it was over. All that clutter that I'd piled and stacked and coated with dust for YEARS came tumbling out, released by a three-word key.

The conversation that followed was as rational as any I'd been having in my own head, but it somehow felt more real. Talking to another human usually does. And just as I'd hoped, taking my mother into my confidence added a level of accountability that I'd been sorely lacking, and it was the thing that ultimately motivated me to get well. It's like how people behave differently when they know they're on camera — I'd turned the lens of someone else's concern and judgement onto myself, and when I was tempted to regress, I remembered that she was watching. I thought about how sad and disappointed she would be to know I was harming myself, and I thought about how happy she would be to know I was getting better.

So yes, mental decluttering is usually a solo mission —
but it doesn't have to be. **If you're struggling to the point
that no combination of strategy, focus, and commitment
can keep the shitstorm at bay, it's perfectly okay to bring
in reinforcements.**

Some of them hold prescription pads; others just hold
your best interests close to their hearts.

Want to make big life changes?
Look at the small picture.

You might be surprised at how often I look back on the
unhealthy/unhappy times in my life. It's not because I
enjoy wallowing in the residue of my adolescent angst or
because I miss corporate life EVEN A LITTLE BIT, but
because getting through those times has shown me that
when I put my mind to something, no matter how major,
I really can make it happen.

Pitfalls in the Game of Life — such as poor time management, distraction, and fear of failure — are identifi-
able. The methods for counteracting or avoiding them are

simple; by now, you should be able to strategize like Garry Kasparov and focus with one arm tied behind your back (you need the other one to hold your phone).

The actual act of commitment is the hardest part, but when you want it badly enough — as I've wanted to get healthy and happy at various times in my life — it's absolutely, positively, 100 per cent doable.

Because big life changes are made in small, manageable chunks.

I've been saying it all along.

Just as you would when confronted by an intricate colouring book page featuring four unicorns frolicking in a wildflower meadow, you have to start somewhere. Maybe the hooves.

Moving across the world, or across the country, or even across the street doesn't happen in the blink of an eye. It starts with motivation, proceeds to goal stage, then into strategy and so on. **A little bit at a time.** Eventually you have one unicorn flank and a few daffodils under your belt, and with those come added clarity — of purpose and of method.

You definitely still want to move to San Diego, you know what neighbourhood you want to be in, and you have your budget, so the next step is what—surfing Gumtree for roommates? Calling real estate brokers? Whatever it is, you carve out some time to focus, commit, and cross it off your list. One hoof in front of another, until all the blank spaces are accounted for (including the change-of-address forms, which are a real pain in the ass, let me tell you).

Or, say you look in the mirror every day and see a twenty-five-years-younger version of your dad en route to quadruple bypass surgery and a medicine cabinet full of blood pressure pills. The good news is, you have a quarter of a century to change course, but the reality is: It starts with one day. Maybe even one second—the second in which you think *Strudel is nice*. And every second you sacrifice to chowing down on that nice hunk of strudel is one less standing between you and an ER nurse with extremely cold hands. She's like a yeti, this woman.

That big swathe of meadow? That's your commitment to a weekly exercise regimen. All green. Fill it in.

And I don't want to sound unaccountably woo-woo here, but the same principles hold true for the deep shit, and **making profound change inside yourself.** Becoming more confident or less of a perfectionist might sound like a tall order, but if you let the perceived enormity of a change keep you from even starting, you won't get anywhere. **Proven fact: You cannot finish something you never start.** Relationships flourish one gesture at a time. Addictions are curbed one day at a time. And unicorns are just horses if you never colour in their horns.

Your goal — the big picture — will reveal itself even if you scribble outside the lines a bit, or use an unconventional shade. The overall effect might be a little different for you than it would be for your cousin Paul, but you're out to win your life, not his.

> **Stretching update, day 30**
>
> This morning I discovered I could stretch without getting out of bed. Life-changing!

Of course, **I'm not saying you should make big changes just for the hell of it.** You may already be winning at *your* life once all the small shit is squared away. But if you feel like what you really need in order to be happy is to radically alter some aspect of your existence — be it your geographical location, body, or baseline mentality — **I *am* saying that those changes are there for the making.**

And just to make sure I don't lose anyone in the deep

shit, let's take a step back and look at how a bunch of small changes can add up to a winning streak of their own.

B-I-N-G-O

Though it has yet to be published in book form, my friend Joe has his own system for getting his shit together. A long time ago, he decided that if he does two out of these three things on any given day, he wins at life:

Floss

Work out

Refrain from drinking alcohol

If he does all of them, that's swell, but just two is enough to pass. Fiddle the old chompers in the AM, and he's clear for an after-work G&T. Skip the workout? No worries, just tend to the fangs and keep his powder dry for one day. It works for him, and I respect that. In fact, I respect it so much, I've adapted his handy-dandy life-hack into one of my own. I call it GYST BINGO. You can cut it out and carry it around in your pocket, which, it pleases me to say, would take "playing with yourself" to a whole new level.

Each square on the GYST BINGO board represents one of these ten small steps toward having your shit together:

Saving or not spending money	Delegating
Being on time	Being selfish (in a good way)
Taking one step toward a goal	Exerting willpower
Prioritizing	Not losing your mind
Controlling an impulse	Not being an insuffer-able prick

They're scattered around randomly so you don't have to do all of them in the same day, nor in the same week. But if you do *enough* of them each day and week, you can score at least one GYST BINGO by the end of the month — maybe several. Let's hear it for fun, interactive takeaways!

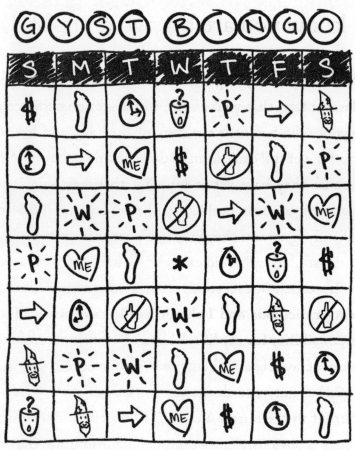

GYST BINGO

#	SAVING / NOT SPENDING
⊕	BEING ON TIME
⎆	ONE STEP TOWARD GOAL
⫶P⫶	PRIORITIZING
⎆	CONTROLLING AN IMPULSE

⇨	DELEGATING
♥ME	BEING SELFISH (GOOD WAY)
⫶W⫶	EXERTING WILLPOWER
⎈	NOT LOSING YOUR MIND
∅	NOT BEING AN INSUFFERABLE PRICK

I know you are but what am I?

The end is in sight, guys. You're almost there. You're so close, in fact, that you've come to the section designed for anyone who bemoans the state of their life and has read this far, yet *still* can't seem to do anything about it. Why? Because they have yet to pinpoint their *own behaviour* as the cause of their problems. They're not dumb or even willfully ignorant; **they just aren't very self-aware.**

Pssst..."they" could easily be "you."

It's cool, not everyone is born with the gene for **"I'm being ridiculous and I should really take stock of and responsibility for my life choices."** But if you're lacking a sense of awareness about your own actions, it's a lot harder to get your shit together than if you can look at yourself in the mirror and say, "Wow, the way I'm doing things is obviously not working. I am losing the Game of Life and honestly, it's all my fault."

So at long last, this is the part of the book where **I'm going to get judgy.**

And so are you.

The final question of my survey was "Name something

OTHER people do that makes you think they don't have their shit together." Someday, I will perform the list of responses in their entirety, perhaps as a one-woman show titled *The Get Your Shit Together Monologues*.

For now, though, we're just going to use them as inspiration. The following is a fun exercise designed to help you win at life by identifying other people's bad behaviour and learning from it. Sometimes, you have to get all lubed up on schadenfreude before you can come around to the thought *Oh shit, I do that too.*

It works like this:

I'm going to give you a list of complaints taken directly from my survey responses.

You're going to match each complaint with a person in your life who is guilty of this behaviour.

You're going to think about how *obvious* it is that they are engaging in self-sabotage to the nth degree, shake your head, mutter *Get your shit together* under your breath, and keep going until you complete the list.

Have fun, I won't tell anyone.

_____ is really disorganized.

_____ is perennially late.

_____ says "that's just how I am," as though that's a valid excuse for always being late.

_____ can never seem to keep a promise.

_____ is in a bad relationship.

_____ is so irresponsible with money.

_____ always talks about starting a diet or workout programme but never follows through.

_____ is so paralyzed by perfection, he/she never gets anything done.

_____ puts everything off until the last minute, then does a shitty job at it.

_____ is impossible to pin down/never commits to anything.

_____ is always spending money he/she doesn't have and is therefore always broke.

_____ complains about his/her job constantly but never looks for a new one.

_____ doesn't take care of him/herself and wonders why he/she feels gross all the time.

_____'s messy home is basically a reflection of his/her messy life.

_____ is so overcommitted, it would be comical if it weren't so sad.

_____ is terrible at responding to emails; it's like they go into a black hole.

_____ keeps doing the same thing over and over, expecting different results.

Now, you're going to stand in front of a mirror and instead of reciting the name of your friend (or family member, colleague, neighbour, or acquaintance) aloud, you're going to substitute **YOUR OWN NAME**.

Every time you experience a twinge of brutal recognition, that's self-awareness. Circle those answers. Meditate on them. **Become the self-awareness you want to see** in your friends/family/colleagues/neighbours/acquaintances.

Congratulations, _____, you just got one (or more) steps closer to winning at life.

Get your shit together, Pam

Out of thousands of responses to my survey, this was my favourite: "When it comes to staying in unhealthy relationships, my friend Pam* is such a drama queen. I always say that when life hands Pam lemons, she goes to the store and buys more lemons."

---

* Name has been changed to protect not-Pam.

Hello from the other side

Q: What do recovering addicts, raw-foodies, and born-again Christians have in common?

A: They're always telling you how great they feel!

Whether holding court at dinner parties or sidling up a little too close to you on the city bus, these Chatty Cathys want you to know their lives are infinitely better now that they've kicked smack, taken up gazpacho, and welcomed Jesus into their hearts. They practically glow from within. You kind of want to kick them in the shins, but you know what? They're winning. Those newly capped teeth, regular bowel movements, and beatific grins could be YOU.

Perhaps that came out wrong.

What I'm saying is, their shit doesn't have to be the same as your shit, but **the principle remains the same: Out with annoy, in comes joy.** Even if you don't agree with these folks' life choices, *believe them* when they tell you how much better everything is now that they've got their shit together.

For a long time, I made the mistake of flat-out not trust-
ing people (in my case: freelancers, including my *husband*) who
told me it was possible not only to live a different kind of life,
but to thrive while doing it. I was sure that even though I was
unhappy in my current existence, throwing a spanner in it
would only make things worse. I was extremely risk-averse,
and those of you who filled out my survey are too.

I got responses like these:

> *I'm stressed and burned out at work and cannot get a break/
> vacation/time off. I hate everything about it and it makes
> me hate life, but I cannot afford to risk leaving.*

> *I want to break up with my current job but have been with
> it a long time and don't have a sweet little thing on the side
> to leave it for.*

> *I've been wanting to leave my job for eleven years.*

Well, thanks in part to the Power of Negative Thinking,
one day my job situation — which looked an awful lot like
each of these examples — became untenable, and something had to give. **The annoy so outweighed the joy that I
had to take action.**

And on the other end, the only person I wanted to kick in the shins was me — FOR NOT GETTING MY SHIT TOGETHER SOONER.

Now tell me, is your annoy off the charts? Is *not* being broke, fat, and messy (or stuck in a dead-end job, or anxious all the time, or constantly out of toilet paper) a goal you can get on board with?

I've said it before and I'll say it again: I don't know your life. I can't set the goal(s) for you. But you can achieve them, one small, manageable chunk at a time. **Keys, phone, wallet.**

And if you're still tempted to keep spinning your wheels in a job or relationship or life you hate, well, consider me Cher to your Nicolas Cage, when I say, "Snap out of it!"

Believe me, the other side is totally worth it. Come on over. You know you want to.

Epilogue

Well, chipmunks, here we are. The end of the road. The final countdown. The cherry on top. You did great! I have one last acorn of wisdom to impart, and then you can gather your metaphorical keys, phones, and wallets and be on your merry way.

Here's the thing: Life is messy. I know this, you know this. We're not fooling ourselves thinking that one little let-me-help-you-help-yourself-help book is going to alter the very fabric of the universe. Even for me, an avid strategizer with hella focus and no trouble with commitment, shit happens.

And you might want to reserve a little time, energy, and money for that scenario, just in case.

Remember that house in the Caribbean? Well, it got built, it is marvellous, and my husband and I sold our apartment, decamped to the DR, and lived there blissfully for three months, giant spiders and all. We hosted friends and family, we walked on the beach, we developed a house cocktail recipe (a Frozen Painkiller, in case you were wondering). We even named our lizards — among them Lizard Khalifa, Senator Elizardbeth Warren, and Jim Morrison. All was right with the world.

Then we came back to New York to settle some final business, in order to complete our goal of moving to the islands once and for all.

Then I had this book idea, and then I sold it to my publisher, and then it was due in ten weeks. *No problem*, I thought. *I'll just get my shit together and write it. I mean, two and a half months? That's an* eternity *compared to last year's deadline! Child's play.*

Except that last year I had an apartment to live in while I was writing my book. This year, I'd sold that apartment to pursue my dream of living on a tropical island, but circumstances demanded that I be off that island and within striking distance of things like "my husband's clients" and "reliable mail services" for a few months, which happened to coincide with my writing time.

No problem, I thought, *we'll secure an apartment, I'll set up my laptop and Diet Coke funnel, and I'll be good to go!*

Only, that little plan didn't quite work out. We drifted like hipster gypsies from an Airbnb to friends' places in Brooklyn and New Jersey, to my in-laws' apartment, to my parents' house in Maine (writing profanity-laced books from your childhood bedroom is one way to spend a summer). Rinse, lather, repeat. I dutifully unpacked and repacked our suitcases every few days, budgeted the increasingly onerous "moving days" into my writing schedule, and kept that word count squarely in my sights at all times.

But the mental clutter was slowly taking up residence in my brain the way my extra luggage was taking up space in my friend's basement.

I tried to keep it contained. I did some deep breathing, indulged my new daily stretching habit wherever we happened to be, and prioritized "self-care" in the form of pizza and pedicures. I wrote and I packed, I wrote and I unpacked.

Finally, the end was nigh.

On the last leg of our Sleeping Around Summer of '16 Tour, I booked another Airbnb that I thought was going to get me through the final stretch of deadline mania and my husband through the last of his business, after which we could ride off into some of the most gorgeous sunsets in the world as reward for jobs well done, and life won.

That's when the shit hit the fan.

I do not wish to cast aspersions on the nice couple who sublet to us, but their apartment was not…to our liking. Some people can live in a perpetually damp, mildew-smelling space, with a cloud of fruit flies for polite company. I am not one of those people. The ceiling fans that we were instructed to "keep on at all times" (to combat the dampness, I assume) produced a *buzz-clank* noise that rapidly achieved Tell-Tale Heart status as I sat under them trying to finish this book. There was no coffeemaker. The final straw was a wiggly millipede thing that I found in the cabinet when I was looking for plastic wrap to create a trap for the fruit flies. If I'm going to live among multilegged fauna, I'm damn well doing it in a tropical oasis, *not* in a basement in Brooklyn.

I'd like to be able to tell you that I handled this situation with grace and aplomb. What actually happened was that I broke down and sobbed on the bed for half an hour while my husband booked a cheap room at a nice hotel on the Hotel Tonight app (bless you, Hotel Tonight app), instructed me to grab my toiletries and pyjamas, and hustled us out of the rental sauna for a restorative night of sweet-smelling sheets and high-functioning AC, with a positively adorable mini-Keurig machine to help me greet the morning.

"We'll deal with the fallout tomorrow," he said. "For now, get some sleep." Small, manageable chunks indeed.

Hallelujah, I thought. *At least one of us has our shit together.*

Then again, he might tell you he learned it by watching me.

GET YOUR SHIT TOGETHER

AND
START
WINNING
AT
LIFE

Acknowledgements

As you now know, most of this book was written while my husband and I were between homes, so I first want to thank the friends and family whose hospitality and spare bedrooms got us through the summer and got me, personally, over the deadline hump.

Thank you to:

Lesley, Cody, Violet, Hayley, and [in utero] Knox Duval, who were the first to put us up and who indeed put up with us multiple times before all was said and done;

Ann and Steve Harris — in-laws extraordinaire — who offered their apartment without hesitation, and

Michael Harris, who provided moral support and exhaustive knowledge of Upper West Side takeout menus;

David Joffe, Katrinka Hrdy, and Mack Hrdy Joffe, who welcomed us with their trademark open arms and mischievous grins;

Steve, Holly, and Gus Bebout, who should definitely be charging more for the Rocky Point Writer's Retreat;

Tom and Sandi Knight, my parents, whose support is consistently expressed by leaving me the fuck alone so I can work, and then feeding me delicious shrimp and opening another bottle of wine;

And two sets of Airbnb hosts who were graciously willing to take our money for weeks at a time. We're batting .500 on that account, but whatever.

Then there are the folks who helped make the life-changing magic happen, *twice*.

Thanks to my agent, the brilliant, chic, and persuasive Jennifer Joel, who has way too many emails in her inbox but never fails to return mine. Her colleagues at ICM, including Sharon Green, Liz Farrell, and Martha Wydysh, are aces.

And thanks to my editor, Michael Szczerban, whose talent for line editing is rivalled only by his enthusiasm for profane punnery. His colleagues at Little, Brown—including but not limited to Ben Allen, Reagan Arthur, Lisa Cahn, Sabrina Callahan, Nicole Dewey, Nicky Guerreiro, Lauren Harms, Andy LeCount, Lauren Passell, Barbara Perris, Alyssa Persons, Tracy Williams, and Craig Young—are selling the shit out of my books, and I'm lucky to have them.

My team at Quercus in the UK—originally led by the delightful Jane Sturrock, who passed the baton during her maternity leave to the kind and perceptive Natasha Hodgson—have had their shit together since Day One. Special thanks to the hardworking trio of Bethan Ferguson, Charlotte Fry, Elizabeth Masters, and new recruit Laura McKerrell. You're the best!

Additional thanks to Ben Loehnen and Kate Whicher for the material, Patrick Smith of Audiomedia Production for engineering my audiobook, and Terry and Manu for getting my iPhone back. It pays to have friends in low places.

Finally, I would be nowhere—least of all sitting under a palm tree sipping margaritas—without Judd Harris. He's the anchor in our relationship relay, and he loves me even when I'm full of shit, which is an excellent quality in a husband.

Index

Page numbers of illustrations appear in italics.

About the Author

 Sarah Knight's first book, *The Life-Changing Magic of Not Giving a Fuck*, was an international bestseller and has been translated into fifteen languages and counting. Her work has also appeared in *Glamour, Harper's Bazaar, Refinery29, Book Riot, Medium*, and elsewhere, though her most widely circulated piece to date is a "Should I Give a Fuck?" flowchart. After quitting her corporate job to start a freelance career and leaving New York in early 2016, she now resides in the Dominican Republic with her husband and a shitload of lizards.

Learn more at sarahknightauthor.com, follow her on Twitter and Instagram @MCSnugz, or read her newsletter at tinyletter.com/sarahknight.

Also available

The surprising art of caring less
and getting more

"A beautiful way of streamlining your psyche" *Guardian*
"Self-help with an edge" *Vogue*
"Wonderfully liberating" *Red*